国家精品在线开放课程配套教材

国际交流英语教程

主 编 周之南 成 城
副主编 任铭静 马 骏

清华大学出版社
北京

内 容 简 介

本教材共有12个单元，内容涵盖了国际交流的三个主要方面，包括日常交流、学术交流和商务交流。通过观看慕课、教师讲授、课上训练、课外阅读和实践作业等途径，本教材旨在让学生了解并掌握国际交流必备的英语知识和技能，为他们以后参与各类国际交流活动做准备。教材配套的教学建议、PPT课件、练习题参考答案等，读者可登录www.tsinghuaelt.com下载使用。

本教材适用于高校英语文化类选修课，也可供具备一定的英语基础，有国际交流的愿望、机会及需求的学习者和涉外工作者参考使用。

版权所有，侵权必究。侵权举报电话：010-62782989，beiqinquan@tup.tsinghua.edu.cn。

图书在版编目（CIP）数据

国际交流英语教程 / 周之南，成城主编 . —北京：清华大学出版社，2023.11
国家精品在线开放课程配套教材
ISBN 978-7-302-63909-1

Ⅰ.①国… Ⅱ.①周… ②成… Ⅲ.①英语—高等学校—教材 Ⅳ.① H319.39

中国国家版本馆CIP数据核字（2023）第114674号

责任编辑：刘　艳
封面设计：子　一
责任校对：王凤芝
责任印制：曹婉颖

出版发行：清华大学出版社
网　　址：https://www.tup.com.cn, https://www.wqxuetang.com
地　　址：北京清华大学学研大厦A座　　邮　　编：100084
社 总 机：010-83470000　　邮　　购：010-62786544
投稿与读者服务：010-62776969, c-service@tup.tsinghua.edu.cn
质量反馈：010-62772015, zhiliang@tup.tsinghua.edu.cn

印 装 者：三河市铭诚印务有限公司
经　　销：全国新华书店
开　　本：185mm×260mm　　印　　张：16.5　　字　　数：318千字
版　　次：2023年11月第1版　　印　　次：2023年11月第1次印刷
定　　价：68.00元

产品编号：091244-01

前言

当今世界正面临百年未有之大变局,当代中国正处在中华民族伟大复兴的关键时期,中国正以昂扬奋发的姿态走向世界舞台中央,为解决全球性问题贡献着中国智慧。同时,世界各种思想文化交流与交融日益频繁,国际舆论斗争和软实力较量更加激烈。深刻理解当代中国的发展进程,创新知识体系、课程体系与教材体系,培养更多具有家国情怀、全球视野、跨文化交际能力,能够讲好中国故事,传播好中国声音的时代新人,成为中国高等外语教育的新使命。本教材正是基于这个时代背景而编写的。

一、教材特色

本教材主要具有以下特色:

- 本教材在教学设计和教学活动的安排上秉持实用性原则,旨在帮助学生用最短的时间学有所得、学以致用。

- 本教材在素材选择上体现了时代性。编者在教材编写过程中,注重吸收新知识,采用新规范和新标准,保证教材内容与时俱进。

- 本教材在内容编排上强调了趣味性。"兴趣是最好的老师",学生对感兴趣的内容会高度关注、反复推敲,从而留下深刻印象。编者在有声资料输入、图片选择和课堂活动设计上,尽可能做到生动有趣,使学生乐学、好学、善学、勤学。

二、教材结构

本教材分为12个单元,每个教学单元都包含热身活动(Warm-Up)、应知应会

（Points to Remember）、实践活动（Let's Do It!）、工具箱（Tool Box）和补充知识（Do You Know?）五个部分。

热身活动部分旨在引入主题和激发学生的兴趣。通过音视频输入和讨论活动，学生可以了解单元主题，预测学习重点和难点，产生学习兴趣。应知应会部分将单元主题之下的国际交流知识和英语表达方式尽数罗列，便于学生背诵和记忆，内容简单、明确、实用。实践活动部分围绕单元主题，设计了模拟场景，为学生提供了将应知应会部分的知识点进行应用和实践的机会。针对实操性强的教学难点和重点，各单元都设计了五个以上情景式、任务型、产出型的教学活动，教师可根据学生的学习水平和实际需要选择使用。工具箱部分针对各单元的主题，列出了常用口语和写作词汇、表达式与句子，方便学生随时查阅、使用和记忆。补充知识部分提供了2～3篇辅助阅读，帮助学生在阅读的过程中拓宽知识面，在提高英语水平的同时，能够掌握国际交流知识。

三、主要内容

本教材涵盖了国际交流实务的主要环节，涉及国际交流活动中的社交、着装、用餐、旅游、住宿、求学、参加或组织国际会议、在国际场合发言、通话、求职面试等方面的文化背景、涉外常识和礼仪规范。

针对上述国际交流场景和实践中的基本要求，本教材提供了全面系统的学习方法、步骤和与之匹配的基本技能训练与指导。

四、配套资源

本教材是国家精品在线开放课程的配套教材，也融合了编者多年讲授国际交流英语课程的教学实践经验，符合信息化、数字化和智能化时代的学习特征。

本教材除了用于线下课堂教学，还配有同名慕课，学生可登录"中国大学MOOC"（累计选课人数近80万人）或"国家智慧教育服务平台"（累计选课人数超100万人），输入"国际交流英语"课程名称，即可选课。学生可以将慕课与本教材的相关章节进行对照学习，以便在不同学习模式中加深对国际交流基本知识的理解与常用英语表达方式的掌握。

本教材的部分练习题配有相应的音频资源，学生可以通过扫描相应的二维码获取。此外，本教材还提供了教学建议、PPT课件和练习题参考答案，读者可登录www.

tsinghuaelt.com 下载使用。

五、适用对象

本教材适合我国普通高等学校的本科生和研究生使用，也可以为从事涉外工作和有国际交流需求的读者提供实用性指导，还可以为拟从事国际交流活动、对国际交流感兴趣或自学英语的读者提供帮助。

教材的出版和推广得到了清华大学出版社的大力支持，在此表示衷心的感谢。编者诚挚希望本教材能成为教师教学和学生学习过程中的得力助手，并帮助他们取得更好的教学和学习效果。由于编者的水平和经验有限，教材中的错误和遗漏在所难免，恳请各位专家、读者提供宝贵的反馈和建议，以便教材不断改进和完善。

编者
2023 年 11 月

Contents

UNIT 1
Greetings, Introductions & Gift-Giving

Section I	Warm-Up	2
Section II	Points to Remember	3
Section III	Let's Do It!	6
Section IV	Tool Box	11
Section V	Do You Know?	13

UNIT 2
Dress Etiquette

Section I	Warm-Up	24
Section II	Points to Remember	24
Section III	Let's Do It!	27
Section IV	Tool Box	32
Section V	Do You Know?	35

UNIT 3
Table Manners

Section I	Warm-Up	44
Section II	Points to Remember	44
Section III	Let's Do It!	47
Section IV	Tool Box	52
Section V	Do You Know?	55

UNIT 4
International Traveling

Section I	Warm-Up	64
Section II	Points to Remember	64
Section III	Let's Do It!	70
Section IV	Tool Box	72
Section V	Do You Know?	75

UNIT 5
Accommodation

Section I	Warm-Up	86
Section II	Points to Remember	86
Section III	Let's Do It!	89
Section IV	Tool Box	93
Section V	Do You Know?	96

UNIT 6
Applying for Universities Abroad

Section I	Warm-Up	106
Section II	Points to Remember	106
Section III	Let's Do It!	110
Section IV	Tool Box	113
Section V	Do You Know?	116

UNIT 7
Application Materials

Section I	Warm-Up	128
Section II	Points to Remember	129
Section III	Let's Do It!	133
Section IV	Tool Box	138
Section V	Do You Know?	141

UNIT 8
Studying Abroad

Section I	Warm-Up	152
Section II	Points to Remember	152
Section III	Let's Do It!	156
Section IV	Tool Box	158
Section V	Do You Know?	161

UNIT 9
International Conference

Section I	Warm-Up	168
Section II	Points to Remember	168
Section III	Let's Do It!	171
Section IV	Tool Box	174
Section V	Do You Know?	177

UNIT 10
Public Speaking

Section I	Warm-Up	194
Section II	Points to Remember	194
Section III	Let's Do It!	201
Section IV	Tool Box	205
Section V	Do You Know?	208

UNIT 11
Telephone Etiquette

Section I	Warm-Up	218
Section II	Points to Remember	218
Section III	Let's Do It!	222
Section IV	Tool Box	225
Section V	Do You Know?	227

UNIT 12
Job Interviews

Section I	Warm-Up	236
Section II	Points to Remember	236
Section III	Let's Do It!	239
Section IV	Tool Box	243
Section V	Do You Know?	246

UNIT 1

Greetings, Introductions & Gift-Giving

Learning Objectives

After learning this unit, you will be able to:
- understand the protocol of international communication in basic social situations;
- analyze situations of international communication regarding greetings, making introductions and gift-giving;
- compare the cultural differences in terms of etiquette of greeting, making introductions and gift-giving;
- create personal introductions on the basis of personal information and international communication situations;
- comprehend the value of mutual respect and courtesy in international communication.

Section I Warm-Up

1. How do people greet each other around the world? Listen to "Greetings from Around the World" and complete the following table.

Where they live	How they greet each other
Korea	
Nepal	
France	
New Zealand	
The United States	
Columbia	

2. How do we greet people in China? Write down greeting expressions in China as many as you can, and put them into English if you can.

3. Write down the greeting expressions you have learned in English as many as you can.

UNIT 1 Greetings, Introductions & Gift-Giving

Section II Points to Remember

There are important points to remember and some rules to follow in present-day international communication. The following is a summary of the basics in regard to greeting, making introductions and gift-giving. Referring to these points constantly may help you communicate with international friends more effectively and politely.

Part 1 Greetings

1. **Saying "Hello"**
   - Greeting people by saying "Hello" with a smile is the most effective way. So always remember to combine verbal and non-verbal ways of communication such as smiling and eye contact on international communication occasions.
   - A smile, a nod, a bow, a wave, or a handshake can also serve as a greeting.
   - Besides "Hello", you can choose to use other greeting expressions according to different situations.

2. **Addressing People**
   - Use "Mr." for men, "Mrs." for married women, and "Miss" for single women, adding their full names or family names until you are told other ways.
   - When you are working, or studying in a university, you are surrounded by a lot of people with Ph.Ds. Then using "Dr." is better than "Mr." if the person has a Ph.D.
   - "Professor" is good only when the person is a real professor. If not, he/she will be embarrassed if you address him/her "Professor".
   - When you are not sure if a lady is married or single, it's better to use "Madam" than "Ms.".
   - Position titles and occupation titles are rarely used before names.

3. **Shaking Hands**
   - Begin with an oral introduction of yourself with eye contact and a smile.
   - Keep your hand open and make sure your handshake is a handshake, not a palm-shake or a finger-shake.
   - Be firm but not strong.

- Shake up and down, not back and forth.
- Adjust duration.
- Shake up and down twice or three times.
- End with eye contact and a smile.
- It is customary for a gentleman to wait for a lady to extend her hand for a handshake.

Part 2 Making Introductions

1. **Introducing Yourself to an Individual**
   - Exchange your names.
   - Shake hands or offer other culturally appropriate greetings.

2. **Introducing Yourself to a Group of People**
   - Say your name.
   - Tell people how you'd like to be addressed.
   - Smile and look confident.
   - Have eye contact or use other friendly body language.

3. **Introducing a Friend to Other Friends**
   - Bring your friends together.
   - It's recommended to introduce a man to a woman, a younger person to an older person, a lower ranking to a higher ranking and a client to a business partner.
   - Make necessary introductions.
   - Explain why you want to introduce these people.
   - Stick around and facilitate the conversation.

Part 3 Conversation Topics

1. **Casual Conversation Topics**
   - Weather.
   - Sports.
   - Entertainment.

2. **Campus Conversation Topics**
   - Campus news and events.

UNIT 1 Greetings, Introductions & Gift-Giving

- Classes and lectures.
- Teachers and fellow students.
- Books.
- Music and leisure activities.

3. Topics to Avoid

- Age.
- Salary.
- Expenses or costs of private property.
- Sickness or death.
- Religion.
- Political standing.
- Sexual orientation or sex.
- In the UK, the Royal family.

Part 4   Gift-Giving

1. When to Give Gifts

- On special occasions, such as birthdays, anniversaries, baby showers, weddings, etc.
- On holidays, such as New Year, Valentine's Day, Mother's Day, Father's Day, etc.
- When you want to say thank you, or sorry, or goodbye to someone.

2. What Gifts

- For men: ties, belt buckles, caps or hats, pocket knives, pens, T-shirts, etc.
- For women: candles, scented soap, candies, scarves, tableware, etc.
- For everybody: picture frames, books, CDs, stamps, specially designed souvenirs and art objects, something handmade or hand-written or hand-painted, etc.

3. How to Give Gifts

- First, you should choose a proper gift. Think about the occasion and the recipient of the gift. Ask yourself: Will it be appreciated?
- Then wrap up your gift to make it look nice.
- Write a card to go with your gift, telling the recipient why you give him/her the gift.
- Finally, present your gift with proper expressions for the occasion.

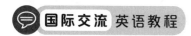

Part 5 Essentials for a Chinese

The following are some additional social etiquette rules to remember when you are in international communication scenarios:

- Make eye contact when you meet/greet/speak to other people.
- Accept and give compliments appropriately and gracefully.
- Be patient. Wait for your turn. Wait for other people to finish talking, eating, entering or exiting the room.
- Express thanks and appreciation properly and duly.
- Observe social rules of other cultures. When in Rome, do as the Romans do.
- Respect other people's privacy. Don't ask questions about other people's private life.
- Help others whenever you can.

And you can add more...

Section III Let's Do It!

Activity 1 Listening About Presents and Bills

There are certain social conventions that British people take for granted but a foreigner may not be aware of. Listen to the recording and find the answers to the following questions.

1. What are the most appropriate presents for a guest to bring to a party?
2. Do you always need to bring something? Or can you just turn up empty-handed?
3. How do people pay for a group meal in a restaurant?

Activity 2 Greetings in Different Situations

1. Think about what greeting expressions are more appropriate on the following occasions. Then fill in the table and discuss with your partner.

UNIT 1 Greetings, Introductions & Gift-Giving

Occasions	Examples	Greetings
Outside & informal	accidently seeing someone on campus or in a street	
Inside & informal	meeting someone at a party, home or in a lab or classroom	
Inside & formal	introducing someone new in an office or a meeting room	

2. Discuss with your partner what expressions are more appropriate when greeting friends, seniors, or juniors.

   Friends: _____

   Seniors: _____

   Juniors: _____

3. What are the similarities and differences between Chinese and Western greeting etiquette? Fill in the table and discuss your answers with the class.

	Chinese Greeting Etiquette	Western Greeting Etiquette
Similarities		
Differences		

Activity 3 Addressing People Properly

When you greet people, you need to address them first. How do you address people in the following situations? Choose the best choice for each situation and share your reasons with the class.

1. Alexander James is a foreign expert working at a Chinese university. You know

him because you are in one of his English speaking classes. When you see him on campus, you should address him as _____.

A. Prof. Alexander James B. Mr. Alexander
C. Mr. James D. Alex

2. Anna Smith is Alexander James' girlfriend who studies for a Ph.D in Chinese at your university. You have seen her with Alexander James hand in hand twice on campus. Now you see her at an English Corner party and you'd like to talk with her. You should address her as _____.

A. Mrs. James B. Dr. Smith
C. Miss Smith D. Anna

Activity 4 Let's Shake Hands!

Everyone in the class shakes hands with the student on the left, then on the right. Remember to use the tips you have just learned. Then go up to your teacher and shake hands with him/her with a one-sentence self-introduction.

Activity 5 Writing a Self-Introduction

1. When you are in a foreign country, you will be frequently asked to introduce yourself. What would you say? Pick out from the following list what must be included in a self-introduction and put a "√" in the box next to the options.

UNIT 1 Greetings, Introductions & Gift-Giving

Options	Must Be Included or Not
Name	
Gender	
Age	
Nationality	
Education	
Hobbies	
Job	
Family	
Religion	
Ethnic origin	
Telephone number	
Email address	

2. Write down a self-introduction of about 5 to 10 sentences in English, covering all the points below about yourself.
   1) Your full name and what you'd like to be called;
   2) Your profile (your job, your education background or your position);
   3) Your special characteristics (which can make people know more about you and remember you);
   4) Your interests (which can help you attract potential friends).

_____
_____
_____
_____
_____
_____
_____

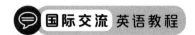

Activity 6　Introducing a Friend

In groups of three, role-play introducing someone to others. The three students in a group take turns to be the introducer, the one to be introduced and the one to listen and respond to the introduction.

Student A's Cue Card:

> You are an international student and you have been here at this university for some time.
>
> A new student from your hometown has just arrived at the same university and you feel it's your obligation to introduce him/her to your supervisor, a very nice native.
>
> Go and knock at your supervisor's office door and try your luck. When introducing your friend to your supervisor, you should:
>
> First, draw your supervisor's attention by politely addressing him/her.
>
> Then, tell your supervisor briefly your friend's name, occupation and relationship with you.
>
> Next, watch them greet each other.
>
> Finally, start up a conversation so that both of them can join in.

Student B's Cue Card:

> You are an international student and you have been at this university for a few weeks.
>
> Everything is new and unfamiliar to you but luckily you have got to know someone who has been here longer. And best of all, you two are from the same hometown!
>
> He/She is going to introduce you to his/her supervisor, a very nice native.

Student C's Cue Card:

> You are a teacher at this university for a long time and you are a native of this place.
>
> You are supervising several international students and you have won their respect by teaching well and helping them when needed.
>
> It's a beautiful day and during your office hours you hear someone knocking at your office door.

Activity 7　Writing a Gift Card

Suppose that you are leaving the university where you have studied for several years. You are so grateful to your supervisor/teacher/friend that you decide to present

UNIT 1 Greetings, Introductions & Gift-Giving

him/her a gift as a souvenir.

Design a card and write what you want to say on it in English. Use the following questions as a reference.

- Who is the recipient? Why do you choose him/her?
- What gift is the best—appropriate, affordable yet meaningful?
- When should the gift be given to him/her? Why?
- What should you say when giving the gift?
- What should be written on the card?

Dear XXX,

_____
_____
_____
_____
_____
_____
_____
_____

With love,

Signature: _____

Section IV Tool Box

1. **Useful Words and Expressions**
   - 令人喜爱的 adorable
   - 讨人喜欢的 agreeable
   - 文明的 civilized
   - 有教养的 educated
   - 举止得体的 gracious
   - 令人愉快的 pleasant
   - 有礼貌的 polite
   - 粗野的 boorish

- 不礼貌的 impolite
- 死板的 rigid
- 不讲究的 rough
- 无礼的 rude
- 情况 circumstance
- 情境 situation
- 祝贺 congratulation
- 礼节 courtesy
- 感激 gratitude
- 正直 integrity
- 个性 personality
- 社交礼仪 social etiquette
- 关系水平 level of relationship
- 认为……是理所当然的 take something for granted
- 入乡随俗 When in Rome, do as the Romans do.

2. **Useful Sentences**

1) Greetings
- Hi.
- Hello.
- How are you?
- How are you doing?
- What's up?
- How do you do?
- Good morning/afternoon/evening!

2) Making Introductions
- I really want you to meet my friend Bob.
- I'm going to introduce you to this person that I think you'll like.
- Good morning, I'm Jennifer Zhou.
- Nice to meet you.
- How is everyone doing today? My name is Lisa Lu.
- My name is Robert Li and I study Computer Science at Cambridge.
- This is Mary Chang, a friend of mine. She studies Education at Stanford.

UNIT 1 Greetings, Introductions & Gift-Giving

3) Small Talks
   - A: Beautiful day, isn't it!
     B: Yes, it is.
   - A: It's awfully hot/cold today!
     B: Yeah, I hope the weather will be fine tomorrow.
   - A: I like jogging/swimming/taking a long walk.
     B: Me, too. It's healthy and easy to perform.
   - A: There's a nice cinema/theater/art gallery/park/garden/tea-house/restaurant/coffee bar near our department.
     B: Oh, yeah? Let's check it out sometime.
   - A: The lecture was great!
     B: Agreed. I like the Q&A session best.
   - A: I'm a huge fan of Dr. XXX.
     B: I bet you are. He/She is the best teacher I have ever known.
   - A: I once read a book about the topic you are working on.
     B: Great! Can you send me the title or the link? Thanks.

4) Giving Gifts
   - Happy Birthday/Anniversary/Mother's Day/Father's Day! Here is my gift to you.
   - Happy New Year! This is a gift from me. I hope you like it.
   - Congratulations! Here is a gift. Open it!
   - This gift is a token of my gratitude. Thank you for helping me!

Section V Do You Know?

Supplementary Readings

Read the following three passages and find out more about social etiquette. The answers to the questions at the beginning of each passage can be found through reading.

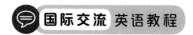

Passage 1 Greetings Around the World

> **Questions:**
> ♦ Why is it important to understand the ways people greet each other?
> ♦ Can you give at least five examples of how people in other countries greet each other?

Customs and rituals involved in greeting others often differ from country to country, and unfamiliar customs can be confusing. Greetings become even more confusing when different greeting gestures are required between male and female, female and female, and male and male. In unfamiliar cultures, travelers may offend others when they meet and greet.

In the United States, men and women shake hands when they meet. Greetings are often casual, such as a handshake, a smile or a "Hello".

The British say "Hello" when they meet friends. They usually shake hands when they meet for the first time. Social kissing or kissing on the cheek is common between men and women and between women who know each other very well.

The Hebrew greeting is "Shalom". The French greeting is "Bonjour".

The Spanish greet with "Hola" and the Zulu say "Sawubona" when greeting friends.

"Namaste" is a greeting in Hindi which translates to "I honor the place in you where the entire universe resides; I honor the place in you of light, of love, of truth, of peace; I honor the place in you where if you and I are in that place then there is only one of us".

In New Zealand, people are often greeted by the Maori leaders with the traditional "Hongi" by rubbing noses.

When a younger person greets an older person in the Philippines, the younger person bows and holds the right hand of the older person and press the knuckles against their forehead. When their knuckles touch the forehead they say "Mano" (means "hand") and "Po" (means "respect").

UNIT 1 Greetings, Introductions & Gift-Giving

The French shake hands with their friends and often kiss them on both cheeks upon meeting and departing.

In Japan, the most common way to greet someone when they meet is to bow. The deeper the bow, the higher the level of respect.

In Arab countries, close male friends or colleagues hug and kiss on both cheeks. They only shake hands with the right hand, which lasts longer but less firm than in Western countries. Physical contact like handshake between men and women in public is considered rude.

Hungarians use the friendly greeting of kissing each other on the cheeks. The most common way to kiss is from your right to your left. When men meet for the first time, they shake hands firmly.

In Belgium, people kiss on one cheek when they meet.

If it is in a formal business situation, Chinese people usually nod, smile or shake hands when they meet someone for the first time.

In Russia, a typical greeting is a very firm handshake while maintaining direct eye contact. When a man shakes hands with a woman, the handshake is less firm. A man can also kiss a woman three times on cheeks alternately.

In Albania, men shake hands when greeting each other. Depending on how well the men know each other, kissing on each cheek is common as well. When a man meets a female relative, he usually gives her one or two kisses on each cheek. When meeting friends or colleagues, normally a gentle handshake is appropriate. Women may shake hands or kiss each other on both cheeks.

In Armenia, a woman needs to wait for the man to extend his hand for a handshake. Among close friends and family members, cheek kissing and light hugs are also common.

Always remember that you are a guest in another country. Please show respect for their customs and culture.

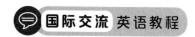

Passage 2 Conversation Etiquette

Questions:
- What should you do before you speak to someone?
- What is the best way to get to know someone?
- What can you do when you can't prevent the conversation from turning into an uncomfortable topic?

Everyone knows someone who speaks out of turn, says the wrong thing that creates an awkward moment, asks rude questions, or never allows others to interrupt. He might have good intentions, but being around him can be upsetting. Don't be that kind of person. If you already are, you probably know it, but you're not sure how to change. It's important to learn some basic social skills and put them into practice.

Regardless of how smart or witty you are, sometimes you need to stop and evaluate the appropriateness of what you are saying. Make sure you have good speech filters to prevent you from saying something rude. To become a good conversationalist, there are some fundamental guidelines you need to learn and practice.

Fundamental Guidelines

1) Pause. Before you say anything, stop and think about what you are going to say. Too many people speak before they think and when the words come out, they don't convey the intended meaning. Before you say anything, pause for a moment and let your internal speech filters take over. This may make a difference whether you're considered as a good conversationalist or a boorish person.

2) Pay attention to signals. As you chat with others, pay close attention to their body language signals that let you know that you are losing them in the conversation. If you continue talking long after they have mentally zoned out, you may find yourself alone, or worse, uninvited to the next get-together. When you realize you've said too much, take a break and give someone else a chance to talk.

Signals that the other person is no longer engaged in the conversation are:

- Yawning.

UNIT 1 Greetings, Introductions & Gift-Giving

- No more eye contact.
- Glancing around the room as if looking for an exit.
- Backing away.
- No response.
- Tapping foot or pointing foot toward the nearest exit.

3) Listen to others. One of the best ways to make people think you are good at conversation is to listen to what they have to say. You should listen without talking and be engaged. This shows that you are interested in what they are saying, and they are more likely to be interested in you when you speak. Give the other person your undivided attention. Listening is the best way to get to know someone.

The following are some ways to show that you are listening:

- Maintain eye contact.
- Nod or occasionally interject, "Yes, I agree" or "I know what you mean".
- Ask questions during pauses.
- Acknowledge and congratulate others on their successes.

Conversation Topics

Before you go to a party or casual get-together with friends, take some time to think about conversation topics. Doing so will help prevent a conversation from getting cold, and you'll find that these topics provide excellent springboards for a conversation that can go in a variety of directions.

The following are some ideas for conversation topics:

- Local news.
- Favorite foods.
- New businesses in the area.
- Sports.
- Hobbies.
- Music releases.
- Favorite books.
- Pop culture topics.
- TV shows or movies.

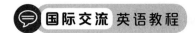

Some topics should be avoided (unless you are with friends who you've known for a long time and will love you anyway):

- Political opinions—unless you are at a political rally or convention.
- Lifestyle pet peeves—unless you are at an event that promotes a specific lifestyle.
- Age issues—unless you are at an event where everyone is the same age.
- Weight issues—unless you are with a group of people whose goals are to gain or lose weight.
- Personal finance—unless the other person is your financial advisor or banker.
- Nitty-gritty details about a health problem—unless you are with a group of health professionals who don't get grossed out from talking about blood and other body fluids.

Etiquette Mistakes

A social situation calls for knowing how to avoid making mistakes in a conversation. Many people wonder what they said or did turned people away. Be aware of some of the most common mistakes that can bring a conversation to a screeching halt.

The following are some common blunders:

- Not knowing anything about the person you are talking to. The solution is simple: take time to get to know the person you are having a conversation with. This will enable you to talk about something that might interest him/her.
- Texting or constantly checking your phone for messages. No one wants to feel that checking the phone is more important than the here-and-now conversation.
- Using R-rated (the "R" stands for "Restricted") language in a G-rated (the "G" stands for "General Audiences") situation. It is just downright rude and offensive.
- Telling off-color jokes. If you don't know the person you are speaking with very well, you never know what might be offensive.
- Interrupting or monopolizing the conversation. Give the other person a chance to shine. If you don't, people will give you a wide berth.
- Randomly changing the conversation to suit yourself. If you do this often,

UNIT 1 Greetings, Introductions & Gift-Giving

others may consider you to be narcissistic.
- Glancing past the person you are speaking to. You don't want to appear opportunistic at the expense of the other person's feelings.
- Acting like a know-it-all. No one knows everything, so don't pretend that you do.
- Forgetting to introduce others. Be gracious and at least start with an introduction.
- Gossiping about others. You never know whose best friend you are talking about.

There are times when you can't prevent the conversation from going toward an uncomfortable topic, and there are a couple of ways you can handle it. You can quickly change the subject and hope the other person takes the hint. Or you can simply say, "Let's not discuss this anymore."

Passage 3 Gift-Giving Etiquette in Chinese Culture

Questions:
- What is important about gift-giving in Chinese culture?
- How much money should be enclosed in a red envelope in China?

In Chinese culture, not only is the choice of gift important, but so is how much you spend on it, how you wrap it, and how you present it.

When to Give a Gift

In Chinese societies, gifts are given on holidays, birthdays, formal business meetings, and at special events, such as dinner at a friend's home. While giving red envelopes is a more popular choice for Chinese New Year and weddings, gifts are also acceptable.

How Much to Spend on a Gift

The value of the gift depends on the occasion and your relationship with the recipient. In business settings where more than one person receives a gift, the person of the highest rank should receive the most expensive gift. Never give the same gift to people of different ranks in the company.

While there are times when expensive gifts are necessary, exorbitant and lavish gifts may not be well received for several reasons. First, the person may be embarrassed that he/she cannot reciprocate with a gift of similar value, or that in business deals, especially with politicians, it may be seen as a bribe.

When giving a red envelope, the amount of money inside depends on the situation. There is a great debate over how much to give.

The amount of money in red envelopes given to children during Chinese New Year depends on the age of the child and the giver's relationship with the child. For younger children, the equivalent of about $7 dollars is fine.

More money is given to older children and teenagers, which is usually enough for the children to buy themselves a gift, such as a T-shirt or DVD. Parents may give the child a more substantial amount since material gifts are usually not given during the holidays.

For employees at work, the annual bonus is typically equivalent to one month's wage, though the amount can vary from enough to buy a small gift to more than one month's wage.

If you go to a wedding, the amount of money in the red envelope should be equivalent to a nice gift given at a Western wedding. The money should be enough to cover each guest's expenses at the wedding. For example, if the wedding dinner costs the newlyweds US$35 per person, then the money in the envelope should be at least US$35.

Generally speaking, the amount of money depends on your relationship with the recipient—the closer you are to the bride and groom, the more you need to give. Immediate family members like parents and siblings give more money than ordinary friends. It is not uncommon to invite business partners to weddings. Business partners often put more money in the red envelope to strengthen the business relationship.

Less money is given for birthdays than for Chinese New Year and weddings because birthdays are viewed as the least important of the three occasions. Nowadays,

UNIT 1 Greetings, Introductions & Gift-Giving

people often just bring gifts for birthdays.

In any case, certain amounts of money are to be avoided. Anything with a four on it is best avoided because 四 (sì, four) sounds similar to 死 (sǐ, death). Even numbers, except four, are better than odd numbers. Eight is a particularly auspicious number.

The money inside a red envelope should always be brand new. Folding the money or giving dirty, wrinkled money is in bad taste. Coins and checks are better avoided, because coins are seldom put into red envelopes and Chinese people are not used to using checks in their daily life.

How to Wrap the Gift

Chinese gifts can be wrapped with wrapping paper and bows, just like gifts in the West. However, some colors should be avoided. Red is lucky. Pink and yellow symbolize happiness. Gold stands for fortune and wealth. So wrapping paper, ribbons and bows in these colors are the best. Avoid white, which is used in funerals and connotes death. Black and blue also symbolize death and should not be used.

If you attach a greeting card or gift tag, do not write in red ink as it signifies death. Never write a Chinese person's name in red ink as this is considered unlucky.

If you are giving out red envelopes as gifts, there are a few points to remember when wrapping red envelopes. Unlike Western greeting cards, Chinese New Year red envelopes are usually unsigned. For birthdays or weddings, short messages, typically four-character expressions, and signatures are optional. Some four-character expressions appropriate for wedding red envelopes are 天作之合 (tiān zuò zhī hé, marriage made in heaven) or 百年好合 (bǎi nián hǎo hé, happy union for one hundred years).

How to Present the Gift

It is best to exchange gifts in private or among a group of people. At business meetings, it is impolite to offer a gift to only one person in front of everyone else. If you have only prepared one gift, you should give it to the person in the most senior position. If you are not sure whether giving a gift is appropriate, say the gift is from your company, not from you. Always give the gift to the person in the most senior position first.

Don't be surprised if your gift is soon reciprocated with a gift of equal value as this is the Chinese way of saying thank you. If you are given a gift, you should also give something of equal value in return. When giving the gift, the recipient may not immediately open it because it would make him/her feel embarrassed or seem greedy.

Most recipients will first politely decline the gift. If someone profusely refuses the gift, take the hint and don't insist.

When giving a gift, hand it to the other person with both hands. The gift represents the good intension of the giver and handing it over with both hands is a sign of respect. When receiving a gift, also accept it with both hands and say thank you.

After receiving a gift, it is customary to say thank you in person or via text message to show your gratitude for the gift. A phone call is also acceptable.

UNIT 2

Dress Etiquette

Learning Objectives

After learning this unit, you will be able to:
- learn about essential etiquette of dressing in international communication;
- learn about basic rules concerning business casual and semi-formal dressing;
- know how to dress appropriately for a job interview and tie a Double Windsor Knot;
- learn about how to dress appropriately as a student and young professional in a different culture.

Section I Warm-Up

1. On what occasions should people dress formally or informally respectively?
2. Dressing is an important factor in a successful job interview. How should people dress appropriately for a job interview?
3. What are the rules of wearing a tie?

Section II Points to Remember

There are important points to remember and some rules to follow in present-day international communication. The following is a summary of the basics in regard to casual and informal dressing, how to dress for a job interview, and how to tie a Double Windsor Knot. Referring to these points constantly may help you portray a competent and confident image in international communication.

Part 1 Casual and Informal Dress

1. **Different Dressing Occasions**
   - Weekend outings with friends.
   - Social occasions.
   - At home.
   - In informal business settings.

2. **Business Casual Attire Etiquette for Men**
   - Shirts: long-sleeved.
   - Watch: conservative.
   - Shoes: leather.

3. **Business Casual Attire Etiquette for Women**
   - Skirts: casual skirts or pantskirts.
   - Sweaters: cotton, silk, or blended.
   - Watch: conservative.
   - Jewelry: keep it simple and avoid dramatic colors or styles.

- Makeup: natural looking.
- Nails: keep them clean and avoid long nails or shiny nail polish.
- Purse: simple and color-coordinated with your shoes.
- Shoes: coordinate with your other attire.

4. Semi-casual Attire for Men
   - Full suit: optional with vest.
   - Tuxedo: not necessary.
   - Tie: should be worn.
   - Shirt: simple button-down.

5. Semi-casual Attire for Women
   - Dress.
   - Dress suit.
   - Pant suit.
   - Cocktail dress.
   - Heels in colors that match the outfit.

Part 2   Dress for a Job Interview

1. Basic Interview Dress Rules for Men
   - Tie: with a conservative style, color and pattern.
   - Tie accessories: tie bars and tie clips.
   - Suit: in a dark color (black, blue, brown and gray).
   - Shirt: in white or pale blue.
   - Belt: in a dark color that matches the color of the shoes.
   - Shoes: conservative in color and polished.
   - Socks: dark in color.

2. Basic Interview Dress Rules for Women
   - Dress or skirt suit: modest and flattering .
   - Pant suit.
   - Neckline: well above the cleavage.
   - Vests and scarves: add an acceptable flair to your outfit.
   - Legs: best covered with pantyhose.

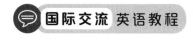

- Shoes: open-toed shoes are never acceptable.
- Less jewelry.

Part 3   Double Windsor Knot

- The Double Windsor Knot is also called the Full Windsor Knot. It is the most popular and fashionable tie knot in the United States. To tie a Windsor Knot, follow these steps:
- Step 1: make sure that the wide end of the tie hangs down much lower. Cross the wide end of the tie over the narrow end and hold in place with two fingers.
- Step 2: take the wide end of the tie and pull it through the loop around your neck. Then take the wide end and wrap it back behind the narrow end.
- Step 3: take the wide end of the tie and pull it through the loop around your neck again from the other side of the previous wrapping.
- Step 4: slightly tighten it and pull the wide end back over the front of the knot. Don't pull tight but create a loop.
- Step 5: pull the wide end of the tie through the loop at the front of the knot.
- Step 6: slightly tighten the knot. Make sure that the wide end of the tie lies in the middle and doesn't fall into the gap created by the two wrappings.
- Step 7: give the knot some final adjustments and flip down your collars. The Double Windsor Knot is done.

Part 4   Essentials for a Chinese

What Not to Wear

◇ Skirts and Shorts That Are Too Short

Many times, women get a bad reputation for the clothes they wear, such as skirts, dresses or shorts that are too short, or shirts and blouses that are too low-cut. Skirts and shorts don't have to be worn below the knees, but a college student should have the good judgment to know when she is wearing them too low.

◇ Wrong Pants

This rule generally applies to males: keep your pants up to the waist! Use a belt or simply buy pants that fit you so your underwear doesn't show and you don't end up

pulling your pants up all day long.

Some females have to be told the same as well: if you can't bend over without showing your unmentionables, then your pants are too low.

What to Wear

◆ Appropriate Clothes

Research the city in which your college is located to see what kind of clothes are appropriate for you most of the year.

Simply dress appropriately according to the season. Wear thin, light-colored clothing in the hotter seasons and thicker, more layered clothing during the cooler season.

◆ Clean Clothes

Select clothes that are wrinkle-free and clean. If you don't like to iron, fold or hang up your clothes so they don't wrinkle.

◆ Shoes

Select appropriate and comfortable shoes, as you'll most likely be doing a lot of walking on campus. Some schools have large campuses, while others have rolling hills.

◆ Business Attire

If you've never worn business attire before, try to buy some. It is not uncommon for professors to require you to dress up for presentations. Buy a suit with a collared dress shirt; usually, they're neutral colored—black, gray or navy blue. Wear appropriate shoes, not open-toed shoes.

Section III Let's Do It!

Activity 1 Making a Conversation About Clothes

This exercise has two sets of questions about clothes and each set has 5 questions. You should use them to have a conversation with your partner. One person takes Set A and the other person takes Set B, then you take turns asking each other questions. Once you have finished, you can switch the questions and have the conversation again. Give detailed reasons for your answers.

	Question Set A	Question Set B
1	Do you think the way people dress is important?	Do you prefer to wear smart or casual clothes?
2	What are your favorite clothes to wear?	Would you like to work in a clothing store? Why or why not?
3	How many clothes do you have?	How often do you change the clothes you wear?
4	Do you prefer bright clothes or dark ones?	What are the most comfortable clothes to wear?
5	Do you spend a lot of money on clothes?	Do the clothes you wear change how you feel?

Activity 2   Describing Formal Clothes and Special Costumes

Work in pairs. Each of the students choose a cue card and describe formal clothes and special costumes, then switch cue cards.

Student A's Cue Card:

You are going to describe an occasion when you wore formal clothes.
You should include:
1) What was the occasion?
2) When did it happen?
3) Where was the location?
4) Why did you need to wear formal clothes?

Student B's Cue Card:

You are going to talk about special costumes.
You should include:
1) Do you like to wear special costumes?
2) Did you try any special costumes when you were young?
3) When was your last time to wear special costumes?
4) Do you ever buy special costumes?

UNIT 2 Dress Etiquette

Activity 3 Comparing Between Fashion and Style

Read the following passage about fashion and style. Try to figure out the differences between them and fill in the table.

> Fashion and style are two common terms which are now vastly used by the young generation. "Fashion is about dressing according to what's fashionable. Style is more about being yourself," said Oscar de la Renta.
>
> **What Is Fashion?**
>
> Fashion is very trendy, which can be seen in magazines, on TVs, and on the fashion runways. In another view, fashion is also the newest creations of designers, which are bought by only a few people. Fashion can be anything, such as clothes, shoes, cosmetics and accessories, which are made popular by fashion houses, models, actors and actresses.
>
> **What Is Style?**
>
> Style is something that is unique to everyone. Style is the person's own choice in clothes, accessories, and others. Style is not totally dependent on clothing; it relates to anything that makes a person look stylish. In another view, style is the extension of fashion which does not change like fashion.

	Fashion	Style
1		
2		
3		
4		
5		

Activity 4 Debating over School Uniforms

Divide the whole class into two teams, and have a debate over the topic: *It is necessary for children to wear school uniforms.* You should follow the debate process and guidelines. Some expressions are given for your reference.

1) Debate Process
   - Divide the class into two debate teams.
   - Preparation: 10 minutes
   - Opening statement (Side A): 4 minutes
   - Opening statement (Side B): 4 minutes
   - Rebuttal (Side A): 2 minutes
   - Rebuttal (Side B): 2 minutes
   - Closing statement (Side A): 1 minute
   - Closing statement (Side B): 1 minute
   - A plenary by teacher/chairperson: 2 minutes
2) Guidelines
   - Listen to the chairperson who leads the debate.
   - Try not to interrupt others.
   - Try to keep your answers short and sharp.
   - Be engaged and ask questions about your opponent's points.
   - Do not touch others.
   - Try to be dispassionate.
   - Do not speak over others.
   - Let your teammates share their ideas as well.
3) Useful Expressions

   For:
   - Wearing school uniforms reduces clothing-related peer pressure.
   - It creates uniformity in appearance among students from different social classes within a school.
   - School uniforms tend to cost less than traditional youth clothing.
   - It can create an environment where discipline is emphasized.
   - It may take students less time to get ready for school every morning.
   - Schools can identify intruders quickly because they aren't in the needed uniform.
   - Uniforms could help students focus more attention on their studies than their fashion.

   Against:
   - It prevents students from showing individuality.
   - It may restrict students' freedom of dress.

UNIT 2 Dress Etiquette

- New school uniforms can be more expensive than traditional clothing.
- Students from low-income families may miss school because they cannot afford uniforms.
- School uniforms can be uncomfortable.
- Creating consistent rules about school uniforms can be difficult.
- Research indicates that there is no relationship between wearing a school uniform or not and studying well.
- School uniform policies can create barriers between students and teachers.

Activity 5 Correcting Dressing Mistakes

Detect the mistake(s) from the following pictures and give your reasons and improvements.

1)

2)

3)
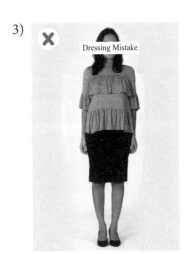

4)

5)

Section IV Tool Box

1. **Useful Words and Expressions**

   1) Nouns
   - 衣服，服装 clothes/clothing
   - （某人的全部）服装 wardrobe
   - 必需品 must-haves
   - 成衣 ready-made clothes / ready-to-wear clothes
   - 衬衫 shirt
   - 女士衬衫 blouse
   - 短袖圆领衫 T-shirt
   - 背心汗衫 vest
   - 马球衫 polo shirt
   - 水手衫 middy blouse
   - 运动衫 sweater
   - 短袖运动衫 short-sleeved sweater
   - 高翻领运动衫 roll-neck sweater
   - 圆领运动衫 round-neck sweater
   - 两件套的运动衫裤 twinset
   - 开襟毛衣 cardigan
   - 帽衫 hoodie

- 休闲西装外套 blazer
- 礼服 formal dress
- 燕尾服 tailcoat
- 晨礼服 morning coat
- 晚礼服 evening dress
- 长袍 gown robe

2) Verbs
- 盛装打扮 dress up
- 适合，合身 fit
- 相配，合身 suit
- 换衣服 get changed
- 穿衣服 get dressed / put something on
- 脱衣服 get undressed / take something off
- 穿，佩戴 wear
- 拉上拉链 zip
- 比平时穿得更为休闲 dress down
- 穿暖和的衣服 wrap up
- 根据场合着装打扮 dress for the occasion

3) Adjectives
- 正式的 formal
- 非正式的，休闲的 casual
- 流行的，时髦的 fashionable
- 过时的，不时髦的 old-fashioned
- 时髦的，赶时髦的 trendy
- 整洁的，漂亮的，穿着讲究的 smart
- 方格图案的 checked
- 有花点的 spotted
- 紧身的，贴身的 tight
- 老式的 vintage
- 定制的 custom-made / tailor-made

2. **Useful Sentences**

1) Commenting on Other People's Outfit Creatively
- You look so confident/happy/glowing.

- I love that so much.
- I've never seen anyone look so ready to own it.
- How do you always come up with such amazing outfits?
- I love the fact that I've never seen something like that on you before!
- You always inspire me to try new things with my clothing.
- Your style is everything.
- That color is great on you!
- I can tell that you love what you're wearing!
- You're absolutely glowing!
- I've been looking for that everywhere.
- You are my fashion hero.
- Wait. Can I take a photo of your outfit? I want to remember it so I can recreate it later.
- I saw that exact look in a magazine yesterday.
- Everyone just turned around to look at you when you walked through the door.
- Tell me where you got every single thing you're wearing right now. Don't spare any details.
- The color of that dress is so incredible.
- You'll be able to wear that everywhere.
- This outfit looks so good on you.
- Where do you get your outfit inspiration? I definitely need to follow those same people.

2) Talking About Company Dress Code

A: Do we have a company dress code?

B: Yes. From Monday to Thursday, we have to wear business attire.

A: What about Friday?

B: On Friday, we can dress casually.

A: What does casual dress mean?

B: You can wear jeans and T-shirts, but not shorts.

UNIT 2 Dress Etiquette

Section V Do You Know?

Supplementary Readings

Read the following three passages and find out more about dressing. The answers to the questions at the beginning of each passage can be found through reading.

Passage 1 The Origin of Neckties

Questions:
- What is the earliest known predecessor of the modern tie? What are the functions of these neck ties?
- What is the second earliest use of neck ties in military history? What is the assumed function of those neck ties?
- What is the third example of neck ties in military history? Why are they believed to be more practical?
- When was the first school tie used?

The necktie has its roots in the military. For starters, a collection of terracotta warriors discovered in Xi'an, China, in 1974 gives us some insight into the style of dress worn by Chinese soldiers over a thousand years ago. China's first emperor, Qin Shi Huang, wanted his army to be buried with him as his guardians in the afterlife. Lucky for all the soldiers involved, his advisers convinced him to have life-size replicas of his troops to serve as his eternal protectors.

In 210 BC when he died, his terracotta army was buried with him. Each statue wore a wrapped neck cloth, the earliest known predecessor of the modern tie. Yet Qin Shi Huang's army seems to have been the

only known Chinese wearers of the neck cloth. There are no known representations of Chinese soldiers or Chinese people in general wearing neckties at this time. So historians believe that these neckties might have been used more or less as badges of honor for Qin Shi Huang's army.

The necktie is also depicted on Trajan's Column in Rome, Italy. Emperor Trajan ruled the Roman Empire from 98 AD to 117 AD. He was regarded as a military genius and was responsible for the greatest expansion of the Roman Empire. His military conquest of Dacia is commemorated on Trajan's marble column erected around 113 AD, showing thousands of soldiers wearing various styles of neckwear. Again, as is the case with the Chinese, there is no record of other Roman soldiers wearing neckties at this time. Thus, some think that the necktie was also a sign of honor befitting exceptional fighters.

During the Middle Ages, another example of the necktie appeared in a military setting. In the early 1630s, during the Thirty Years' War, Croatian soldiers in support of France were presented to the French King Louis XIII. Croats wore colorful, knotted neckerchiefs as a part of their uniforms, which attracted their French partners who were accustomed to wearing starched, ruffled collars. Apart from its decorative purpose, the necktie was more practical than these stiff collars and could protect the soldiers' shirts and buttons. By the time Louis XIV came to the throne, these ties became fashionable in France. Military personnel, French courtiers, and ordinary French people began wearing the accessory in various colors and fabrics. Some people even believe that "cravat", the French word for "tie", was just a corruption of "croat", as the style was adopted from the croats.

Though the cravat is regarded as the true forerunner of the modern tie as a fashion accessory, it took hundreds of years for the tie to evolve into the narrow strip of cloth we think of today as a necktie. The fancy cravat made its way to England after Charles II reclaimed the throne in 1660. Other aristocrats in exile in Europe followed him in wearing the cravat, which became a fashion rage that also spread to the British colonies. The neckwear grew to be a stylish accessory for the well-dressed gentlemen who wore it in every imaginable color and style. There were cravats of tasseled strings, ruffled collars, ribbons, embroidered linen, cotton, and an abundance of lace.

UNIT 2 Dress Etiquette

The trend continued into the eighteenth century when donning a piece of cloth around a man's neck became immensely popular among all men regardless of status. At the end of that century, wearing a black cravat was considered the height of fashion. In 1815, the French Emperor, Napoleon Bonaparte who always wore black, wore a white cravat during the Battle of Waterloo to honor the Duke of Wellington who favored that color in battle. It was also around that time that people began to refer to a cravat as a "tie" for the first time, of course referring to the fact that the cravats were tied around the neck.

Variety in ties, innovation and complexity in knots were the order of the day. Books and pamphlets were written about the subject. In 1818, *The Neckclothitania* was published, using satire to make fun of the elaborate cravat styles. In 1828, H. Le Blanc wrote *The Art of Tying the Cravat*, demonstrating in 16 lessons 32 different styles of cravats.

The Industrial Revolution from the eighteenth to nineteenth centuries was the catalyst that led to the necktie as we know it today. "White collar" workers of the day sought comfort and simplicity over excessively elaborate dress of the past. Stiff, fancy, hard-to-tie neckties had no place in the factory. Men tied their neckwears in a four-in-hand knot, that is, a knot at the throat with two ends of fabric trailing down. This method of tying a knot was much less intricate than wearing a cravat, and the knot remained secure. It remains popular today.

It was also around this time that the idea of wearing a tie to show one's affiliation was developed. In 1880, the first school tie was fashioned when a member of Oxford University Boat Club removed the ribbons from his boater hat and tied them in four-in-hand knots. The trend caught on and ties for various affiliations developed.

In the 1880s, the ascot tie became the standard for formal morning dress. It was made a famous fashion item by Britain's King Edward VII, also known as Bertie, who wore it to horse races and his subjects followed. The name is derived from one of the most celebrated horse racing events in England—the Royal Ascot. The ascot tie, tie and bow tie are still regarded as choices for morning dress today. They were and are still typically decorated with brooches.

By the 1920s, the tie evolved even more drastically when Jesse Langsdorf, a New

York tie maker, cut the fabric at a 45 degree angle using a three-piece construction. The gist of this innovation is that it allowed the tie, when tied in standard knots, to drape evenly without twisting, and gave us the modern look. Since then, over the years the width of tie has expanded and shrunken; the length has grown and shortened; and colors and designs have become brighter and softer, but despite those changes, the style has remained substantially the same. Modern ties are even generally manufactured in the same basic way developed by Langsdorf.

Passage 2 What to Wear to a Graduate School Interview

Questions:
- What is the importance of dressing appropriately for a graduate school interview?
- What are the preferable colors for males' suits?
- What are the policies for choosing shoes and socks/stockings?
- What is the last step before the interview meeting?

Your interview may be one of the best ways to demonstrate your unique personality and presence to the admissions director of your prospective graduate school. Your sense of humor, your wit, your poise and eloquence can easily be undermined or enhanced by the clothes you choose. Selecting appropriate, understated attire will give an impression of professionalism. Outfits and hairstyles that are too casual or too loud can make it easy for an interviewer not to take you seriously. Here are some suggestions for how to dress and primp for your graduate school interview:

What to Wear for a Graduate School Interview

- Choose a suit if you're male, a skirt or pant-suit if you're female. Depending on the setting, you may or may not need a suit jacket, but it's best to keep it with you just in case. Play it safe with colors like black, dark brown, dark blue, or gray. Steer clear of whites, pastels, neons and other bright hues. Women should keep their skirts reach at least to the knees. Men should be careful that pants and sleeves are neither too short nor too long. As with all of your other clothing selections, everything should be clean and neat, with no visible stains

UNIT 2 Dress Etiquette

or raggedy hems.
- Wear a shirt with a collar. Ladies can consider wearing a blouse under a blazer, but to avoid revealing cleavage, and lace clothing is best left at home. You have wide options for color, but it's still best to avoid extremely bright hues.
- Choose conservative shoes to match your outfit. Again, staying with the dark colors is your best bet. Heels should be in good shape and toes should not be scuffed. Match your shoes with neutral socks (men) or stockings (women).
- Accessories should be tasteful. They can have an element of creativity, but avoid anything that might scream "eccentric" or "flashy". When in doubt, don't wear it. You want your interviewer to be looking at you, not your Rolex, 3-carat diamond studs or necklace made of bottlecaps.
- In this day and age, a wide range of hairstyles are acceptable—some men have longer hair, while some women have short hair. Just make sure your hair is clean and neat. It's also suggested avoiding any hairstyle that requires excessive product—think Mohawks—and keeping the color natural (or close to natural) anyway.

What Not to Wear for a Graduate School Interview
- Overwhelming your interviewer with cologne, perfume, or worse, a funky natural smell, is a surefire way to leave a bad impression. We're not saying that you have to avoid scent entirely, but one spray (or dab) is better than three or four. And don't forget that a swig of mouthwash can be your best friend in close quarters. In the end, do you want to be remembered for your dazzling remarks on current events, or for the overwhelming cloud of Drakkar Noir that accompanied you?
- Don't forget your hands and nails! Remember, you have to shake the interviewer's hand, and a clammy grip or razor-sharp nails just won't leave a great first impression. Invest in a manicure, or, at the very least, clip and clean your nails at home. Bring lotion if your hands tend to be scaly and dry, and if your palms sweat from nervousness, wipe them off before the interview.
- Just before your interview, do a last-minute check—make sure everything's tucked in, no wayward belly or back flesh is exposed, and any labels from new items have been clipped. Finally, don't forget your smile. It doesn't mean that

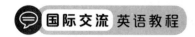

a creepy, plastered-on perma-grin is the way to go, but flashing your pearly whites when meeting your interviewer and when thanking them for their time is polite, and shows your confidence.

- Dressing appropriately for a graduate school interview can help you feel more confident and allow your intelligence and charm to take center stage. Remember you are presenting yourself as a professional who can add value to the program that you are applying for. Keep your interview style neat and simple.

Passage 3 The Effect of Physical Appearance in the Workplace

Questions:
- On business occasions, what are the influences of the way you look on your career?
- How do you understand the statement that "the way employees look impacts the overall feeling of a business".
- How to prepare before meeting potential clients?

Physical appearance can have a far-reaching impact on your career. It can affect how your employers treat you and how much clients put in your abilities, regardless of your actual skill level. Even if your company does not have a published dress code policy, paying attention to what your appearance says about you can benefit your career.

Professionalism

Physical appearance gives immediate clues about your level of professionalism in the workplace. A certain level of neatness is expected in most businesses, even those with very casual dress codes. Sloppy dress and personal presentation imply that you don't care about your job, even if that's not the case. The way you look can affect the way people communicate with you and show your respect.

Company Image

The way employees look impacts the overall feel of a business. Young, trendy employees give the impression of a fast-paced, edgy company; older, more formal employees give a sense of steadiness and experience. Company uniforms and grooming standards exist to manage the overall image of a business. More traditional companies may require employees to remove piercings and cover tattoos. The way you look also has an impact on hiring decisions, especially when your appearance goes against the core values of a business: A fitness center may be hesitant to hire an unhealthy or unfit person.

Client Perception

Employees' appearance is an important consideration when meeting potential clients, especially if the employees look very different from what the clients usually see. Younger employees who do not look professional may worry older clients who will entrust the business with a great deal of responsibility; older, traditional employees may not give off a "cutting edge" vibe to clients looking to move forward. Research new clients before the first meeting to get a sense of their styles and personalities; if your appearance is very different from theirs, be prepared to work harder at the interview to convince them of your abilities and suitability.

Advancement

Conventional wisdom says to dress for the job you want, not the job you've got. According to *USA Today*, the way you look can affect how you advance in your career and how much money you make; people who look better often earn more. People will take clues from your appearance about your ambition, working style and how much you care about your job. If you look put-together and dress appropriately, you may find that employers take greater interest in you, or your colleagues give your ideas more weight.

UNIT 3

Table Manners

Learning Objectives

After learning this unit, you will be able to:
- understand basic Western table manners;
- analyze situations of international communication and know what to do regarding ordering a meal, setting a table, Western dining etiquette and eating at a buffet;
- compare the cultural differences between Western table manners and Chinese table manners;
- introduce Western table manners.

Section I Warm-Up

1. What do you know about Western food? How many courses are there in one dinner? What are they?

2. Describe your experience of having Western food.

Section II Points to Remember

There are important points to remember and some rules to follow when having a Western dinner. The following is a summary of the basics in regard to course serving, table setting, Western table manners, and eating at a buffet. Referring to these points constantly may help you behave well at table.

Part 1 Course Serving

- The first course: appetizer.
- The second course: salad or seafood.
- The third course: soup or sorbet.
- The fourth course: main dish.
- The fifth course: dessert.
- The sixth course: coffee, tea or dessert wine.

UNIT 3 Table Manners

💬 Part 2 Table Setting

- The basic rule for using silverware and dinnerware is from the outside in.
- Eat to your left, and drink to your right.

💬 Part 3 Western Dining Etiquette

1. **Where to Sit**
   - A single table: the host and hostess usually sit at opposite ends facing each other or occasionally in the center of the table.
   - Multiple tables: the host and hostess may sit at separate tables.
   - The highest ranking male usually sits to the right of the hostess.
   - The wife of the highest ranking male or the highest ranking female herself sits to the right of the host.
   - The second ranking male usually sits to the left of the hostess.

2. **How to Eat**
   - It is okay to take a sip of water at the table first.
   - For all other drinks, wait for the host to start.
   - Pass bread or other shared food to the right.
   - Start your meal only when everyone has been served and your host has started eating.
   - Chew with your mouth closed.
   - Don't make loud chewing or slurping noises when eating.
   - Use the napkin to dab or gently wipe at your mouth.
   - Don't pick teeth, blow nose, or reapply lipstick at the table. Go to the restroom.
   - Do not slurp the soup.
   - When eating the soup, tilt the spoon towards your far side.
   - Cut only a few pieces of meat at a time.
   - Thank the host verbally after the meal, and send a handwritten note or email later.

3. **How to Use Utensils**
   - Hold your fork like a pencil.
   - The index finger is extended along the back of the fork, as far from the tines as possible.

- When taking a break from eating, you can rest your utensils in the center of your plate with the tips facing each other in an inverted V shape.
- When each course is finished, you should place the knife and fork parallel with the handles at the four o'clock position on the right rim of the plate.
- The blade of your knife should face inward.

4. How to Drink
   - Follow the lead of the host.
   - If the host has not yet ordered, do not order alcohol.
   - Never order alcohol for lunch.
   - Do not drink excessive amount even if the host does.
   - Wine glasses should be held by the stem.
   - If you're not sure what to do, you can always follow the host.

5. How to Tip
   - Generally, a tip of 15% of the bill is the norm.
   - Tip 20% for very good service.
   - Tip at least 10% for poor service.
   - Don't tip if it's not deserved.
   - If you take up a restaurant table for a long time, tip extra.

Part 4 How to Eat at a Buffet

- Always wash your hands before lining up at the buffet.
- Only move in one direction when fetching the buffet.
- Do not cut into the line.
- Select an appetizer and a salad or a salad and an entrée for your first plate as you pass through the buffet.
- Getting dessert requires a separate plate and another pass through the buffet.
- Do not overfill your plate and do not use the same plate to take food.
- Do not eat food as you pass through the buffet.

Part 5 Essentials for a Chinese

- After entering the restaurant, wait to be seated by the server.

UNIT 3 Table Manners

- Once you're seated, put your napkin on your lap and wait for the server to bring you the menu.
- When ordering, let the server know if you have any dietary restrictions or preferences.
- Speak clearly and confidently when asking for recommendations or making substitutions.
- Start eating only after everyone at the table has been served.
- Remember to use utensils properly.
- If someone offers you food, allow them to serve it to you.
- Don't reach across the table or ask others to pass the dishes to you.
- Don't speak with your mouth full.
- Take small bites and chew with your mouth closed.
- Keep your hands visible on the table and avoid playing with your phone or talking with someone else while eating.
- When the bill arrives, thank the server and leave a tip, usually around 10%–20% of the total bill.

And you can add more...

Section III Let's Do It!

Activity 1 Ordering a Meal

1. Read the following conversation with your partner. Then exchange roles and read again.

   (W: waiter C: customer)
   W: Good morning, sir.
   C: Good morning.
   W: Take a seat, please. Here is the menu. I will come around to take your order a moment later.
   C: Thank you.
   W: Excuse me, sir. Are you ready to order?

C: Yes. I will have the French onion soup and the roast chicken.

W: Yes, sir. Do you wish to take anything else?

C: No, thank you.

W: You order the French onion soup and the roast chicken. I will bring the dishes straight away.

W: This is the chicken. Here is your soup. That is all for your dishes. Enjoy yourself.

C: OK. Thank you.

C: Let me have the bill, please.

W: Here you are, sir. Twenty eight pounds.

C: OK.

W: Thank you. Here is the change.

C: Good bye.

W: Bye.

2. Use the menu below and work with your partner to role-play ordering at a restaurant.

Student A's Cue Card:

- You are a waiter/waitress in the Hill Restaurant in the UK.
- You serve a tourist from China and help him/her to order a meal.
- You can explain the courses on the menu.
- You should work out the total price of the order.

Student B's Cue Card:

- You are a tourist from China and are having a meal in the Hill Restaurant in the UK.
- You are ordering a meal.
- You can ask for help from the waiter/waitress.
- Do not forget to tip.

THE HILL RESTAURANT

STARTERS	**SNACKS (Lunchtime only)**
Tomato Soup £2.0	Burger £3.0
French Onion Soup £2.5	Chicken Sandwich £3.5

UNIT 3 Table Manners

Tomato Salad £3.0
Chicken Salad £3.5

Chocolate Cake £3.5
Cheese Omelet £3.5

All starters are served with bread and butter. All snacks are served with salad and chips.

MAIN COURSES

German Sausage and Chips £7.0
Grilled Fish and Potatoes £6.5
Italian Cheese and Tomato Pizza £5.0
Thai Chicken and Rice £6.5
Vegetable Pasta £5.0
Roast Chicken and Potatoes £6.5

DESSERT

Fruit Salad and Cream £2.5
Ice Cream £2.0
Lemon Cake £2.5
Cheese and Biscuits £2.5

DRINKS

Mineral Water £1.0
Fresh Orange Juice £1.5
Soft Drinks £1.5
English Tea £1.0
Irish Cream Tea £1.0

Lunch Served 12:00–2:30 p.m.
Dinner Served 6:00–9:00 p.m.

Activity 2   Setting the Table

Discuss with your partner how to set the table and draw the following tableware in the blank.

1) water glass
2) wine glass
3) dinner plate
4) bread plate
5) salad fork

6) dinner fork
7) dessert fork
8) dessert spoon
9) soup spoon
10) dinner knife

Activity 3 Practicing Western Dining Etiquette

1. Work in groups to sum up some dos and don'ts of Western table manners and fill in the following table.

Dos	Don'ts

2. Role-play eating in a restaurant with your partner and go to the front to perform.

Student A's Cue Card:

- You eat in a Western restaurant.
- Show us good table manners.

Student B's Cue Card:

- You eat in a Western restaurant.
- Show us bad table manners.

3. Prepare a three-minute speech entitled "How to Behave Well at Table". Present your speech in a small group of 4–5 people. The best in the group should go to the front and make the speech to the class. You can write down key words or the outline of your speech below.

How to Behave Well at Table

Beginning:

_____
_____
_____
_____

UNIT 3 Table Manners

Body:

_____
_____
_____
_____
_____
_____
_____
_____
_____
_____

Ending:

_____
_____
_____
_____

Activity 4　Chinese Dinner vs. Western Dinner

Discuss with your partners several aspects of differences between Chinese table manners and Western table manners. You can check your answers by reading the passage "Chinese Dinner vs. Western Dinner" on Pages 60–62 for reference. Then make a summary and fill in the following table. You can also add points.

Chinese Dinner vs. Western Dinner

	Chinese Dinner	**Western Dinner**
Starter		
Main course		

(Continued)

	Chinese Dinner	**Western Dinner**
Soup		
Dessert		
Where to serve dishes		
Bones		
...		

Section IV Tool Box

1. **Useful Words and Expressions**
    1) Cooking Methods
        - 焗 bake
        - 搅拌，混合 blend/mix
        - 煮 boil
        - 煨 braise
        - 放入热油里炸 deep-fry

- 油煎 fry
- 扒 grill
- 水煮 poach
- 烤 roast
- 蒸 steam
- 炖 stew
- 以某种原料填充 stuff

2) Doneness
- 三成熟的 rare
- 四成熟的 medium rare
- 五成熟的 medium
- 七成熟的 medium well
- 全熟的 well-done

3) Tastes
- 苦 bitter
- 辣 hot
- 咸 salty
- 酸 sour
- 甜 sweet

4) Restaurant Staff
- 经理 manage
- 主管 supervisor
- 厨师长 chef
- 厨师 cook
- 领班 head waiter
- 男服务员 waiter
- 女服务员 waitress
- 接待员 receptionist
- 调酒员 bartender
- 实习生 trainee

2. Useful Sentences

1) Ordering a Meal
- Can I have the menu? / Could you please give me the menu?

- I need a few more minutes to decide.
- Yes. I'd like to have/try some...
- I'll try/have...
- I'd like my steak rare/medium/well-done.
- I can't decide. What's your recommendation?
- What would you suggest? / What do you recommend?
- What's good today? / What are the specials?
- Let me have the bill, please.

2) Taking a meal order
- Can/May I take your order now? / Would you like to order now?
- Do you need a few minutes (to decide what you want)?
- Well, ...is popular and...is good.
- It's delicious and worth a try.
- I do apologize for giving you the wrong soup.
- How do you like the fish cooked this way?
- I'm sorry to have kept you waiting.
- I would suggest Californian red wine for the beef steak.
- What would you like to drink, coffee or tea?
- Thank you. Here is the change.

3) Differences Between Chinese and Western Table Manners
- The most obvious difference is that they use knives and forks, but we use chopsticks.
- We prefer a round table in Chinese banquets. In the West, a long table is the choice in the banquet.
- The dinnerware we use includes chopsticks, small dishes, spoons, bowls and so on. Westerners prefer to use knives and forks, spoons, dishes, glasses and so on. The common principle is that the fork is on the left and the knife is on the right.
- In China, the first courses are cold dishes, beverage and wine, and then the hot dishes; next staple food; at last the sweets and fruit. Western serving steps are usually appetizers, salad, soup, main course, dessert, coffee or tea.

Section V Do You Know?

Supplementary Readings

Read the following three passages and find out more about table manners. The answers to the questions at the beginning of each passage can be found through reading.

Passage 1 Western Table Manners

Questions:
- Where do you put your napkin?
- How do you leave your knife and fork on your plate when taking a break?
- How do you eat soup?
- Where should the guest of honor sit at the table in a restaurant?
- Who clears the plates at a family meal?

Napkin Etiquette

At informal meals, place the napkin on your lap immediately after you are seated. On formal occasions, before unfolding the napkin, wait for the hostess to take her napkin off the table and unfold it on her lap first.

When leaving the table temporarily, put the napkin on your chair.

At the end of the meal, fold your napkin and place it to the left of your place setting.

Holding Utensils

How do you hold a fork?

The continental style prevails at all meals, formal or informal, because it is a natural, non-disruptive way to eat.

- Hold your fork in your left hand, tines downward.
- Hold your knife in your right hand, an inch or two above the plate.

- Extend your index finger along the top of the blade.
- Use your fork to spear and lift food to your mouth.

Resting Utensils

How do you leave your knife and fork on your plate when you take a break or finish eating?

When you pause to take a sip of your beverage or to talk with someone, rest your utensils in one of the two following styles:

- Continental Style: Place your knife and fork near the center of the plate, slightly angled in an inverted V shape and with the tips of the knife and fork pointing towards each other.
- American Style: Rest your knife on the top right of your plate (diagonally) with the fork nearby (tines up).

When each course is finished, you should place the knife and fork parallel with the handles at the four o'clock position on the right rim of the plate.

Passing Food Etiquette

Pass to the right (if the item is not being passed to a specific person). One diner either holds the dish as the next diner takes some food, or hands it to the next person to help himself/herself. Any heavy plate should be put on the table after each pass.

If the loaf is not cut, cut a few pieces and offer them to the person on your left, then pass the basket to your right.

Instead of touching the loaf with your fingers, use the cloth in the bread basket as a buffer to stabilize the bread as you slice it.

Place the bread and butter on your butter plate—yours is on your left—then break off a bite-sized piece of bread and eat it with a little butter on top.

Always pass the salt and pepper together.

Soup Etiquette

Hold the soup spoon by resting the end of the handle on your middle finger, with your thumb on top. Dip the spoon sideways at the near edge of the bowl, then scoop a spoonful of soup towards your far side. Sip from the side of the spoon. To have the last spoonful of soup, slightly tip the bowl away from you.

Seating Etiquette

The host may have seating arrangements in mind, so you should allow him/her to direct you to your seat. As the host, you should suggest seating arrangements.

In a restaurant, the guest of honor should sit in the best seat at the table. Usually that is the one with the back of the chair facing the wall. Once the guest of honor is seated, the host should sit to his/her left. Other people are then offered seats around the table.

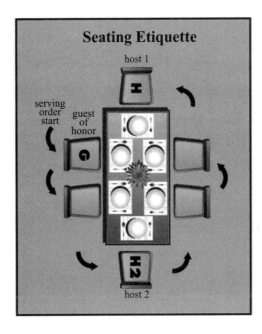

Food Service Etiquette

At a formal dinner, the food is brought to each diner at the table; the server presents the platter or bowl to the diner's left. At a casual meal, either the host puts food on the guests' plates for them to pass around the table, or the diners help themselves and pass food to others if necessary.

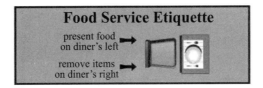

Meals End

At a formal banquet, plates are removed by professional waiters. But as most informal meals are served without help, the hostess will often clear the plates with the help of one or two guests. At a family meal, members clear their own plates.

To signal dinner is concluded, the hostess catches the eye of the host, lays her napkin on the table, and suggests that everyone go into another room for coffee and after-dinner drinks.

When it's time to leave, rather than delaying the host's time with a lengthy good bye, make the departure brief but cordial.

Passage 2 Chinese Table Manners

> **Questions:**
> - Where should the guest of honor sit in a Chinese restaurant?
> - When may the dining begin?
> - What are the no-no's of using chopsticks?
> - What should you do when someone toasts you?
> - Should all the dishes be eaten up completely?

A multitude of etiquette considerations occur when dining in China. There are some special differences between table manners in China and Western countries.

Dining in a Chinese Restaurant

Round dining tables are more popular than rectangular or square ones. Many people can sit comfortably around it and conveniently face each other. The guest of honor is always seated to the right of the host; the next in line will sit on his left. Guests should be seated after the host's invitation, and it is discourteous to seat guests where the dishes are served.

Only when the host and all his guests are seated can the dining begin. The host should actively take care of all his guests, inviting them to enjoy their meal.

UNIT 3 Table Manners

On a typical Chinese dining table, there is always a cup, a bowl on a small dish, together with the chopsticks and a spoon. Dishes are always placed in the center of the table.

Enjoying Delicious Chinese Food

Apart from soup, all dishes should be eaten with chopsticks. The Chinese are particular about the use of chopsticks. There are many no-no's, such as twiddling with chopsticks, licking chopsticks, using chopsticks to stir up the food, gesturing or pointing at others with chopsticks. Never stick chopsticks in the center of rice, as this is the way of sacrifice and is therefore considered inauspicious.

Keep your dining pace accorded with other people. Never smoke when dining.

A formal dining is always accompanied by tea, beer or distilled spirit. The one who sits closest to the teapot or wine bottle should refill for others, from the senior and superior to the junior and inferior. And when other people fill your cup or glass, you should express your thanks. Guests cannot pour tea or wine themselves.

Toasting When Dining Together in China

Toasting to others is a characteristic of Chinese dining. When all people are seated and all cups are filled, the host should toast others first, together with some simple prologue to let the dining start. During the dining after the host and the senior's toast, you can toast anyone according to the order of age or rank at their convenience. When someone toasts you, you should immediately stop eating and drinking to accept and toast in response. If you are far from someone you want to toast, you can use your cup or glass to tap on the table to attract attention, rather than raise your voice. Besides, it is impolite to urge others to drink.

Conventionally, if you are invited to a formal banquet, all the dishes should not be eaten up completely, or you will give the host the impression that he/she does not provide a good banquet and the food is insufficient. After dining, guests should leave once the host has left the table.

Passage 3 Chinese Dinner vs. Western Dinner

> **Questions:**
> ♦ What is the main course in Chinese dinner?
> ♦ How are dishes served in Western dinner?
> ♦ Why are chicken feet and necks not cheap in China?

There are several differences between Chinese dinner and Western dinner, including the dinner procedure, the way of serving, the diet structure, etc.

A Comparison of Dinner Procedure

Western dinner:

- Starter: vegetable salad or soup.
- Main course: The most typical main course would be fillet steak, chicken or fish.
- Dessert: After the main course, usually some sweat food is served, which can be ice-cream, cakes, fruits, pastries, etc.
- Coffee: After the table is cleared, coffee is served. This is usually the very last course.

Chinese dinner:

- Tea
- Appetizer/Starter: Chinese starters are normally cold dishes. The main ingredients of Chinese starters can be vegetables or meat that is cooked and then cooled down. Soy sauce, vinegar, and hot pepper oil are often used in these cold dishes.
- Dishes: In Chinese food culture, many dishes can be ordered if a group of people sit around one table. Types of Chinese dishes are just too many to enumerate. There are eight major regional cuisines in China, each with its own set of typical dishes. Beer, wine or alcohol can be served together with dishes.
- Main course: The Chinese people refer to the main course not as a dish, but as rice or wheat food, such as noodles or steamed buns. This might be a major difference between Chinese food culture and Western food culture.

UNIT 3 Table Manners

This difference is due to the difference in food structure and food concept. In traditional Chinese yin-yang theory, meats are unbalanced in terms of yin-yang. So the Chinese people do not take them as the main course. At a big banquet with a lot of dishes, people may not be able to eat much after having many kinds of dishes, but they normally would still have a small bowl of rice or noodles.

- Soup: Chinese soup is served after main dishes. This is another difference between Chinese food culture and Western food culture.
- Fruits: The most typical desserts in Chinese dinner are fruits. High-quality restaurants often have several types of fruits arranged in beautiful patterns on a large plate. The most favorable fruits might be watermelon and pears, which can make people feel refreshing in the mouth and stomach after the meal.

Serving Dishes at the Center of Table vs. in Each One's Own Plate

One of the biggest differences between Chinese dinner and Western dinner might be the location of the dishes.

In a Western dinner, foods are served in each person's own plate. So each person uses a big plate. When eating in a Western restaurant, everyone orders three courses for themselves.

In a Chinese dinner, dishes are served in the middle of table for all to share, and each person uses a small plate in front of him/her to hold the food picked from the shared dishes. One takes as much as one can eat. This custom also applies to starters/appetizers. However, as for the main course of a Chinese dinner, such as rice or noodles, they are often served to each person separately in a small bowl.

When several people go out for dinner, the Chinese way of eating is helpful to make everyone enjoy a diversified meal, because everyone can order different dishes for all to share.

Chicken Breast vs. Chicken Feet/Necks.

There are some other interesting differences between Chinese food culture and Western food culture.

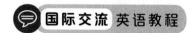

In Western supermarkets, chicken breast is the most expensive of all parts of chicken, while other parts are relatively cheaper. Chicken feet and necks are just discarded and never sold in Western supermarkets.

In China, however, people regard that meat close to the bone is tastier than big chunk of meat. Some Chinese people have special interest in having the small pieces of chicken from the feet and neck. In China, chicken feet and necks are not cheap because a reasonable number of feet and necks can only be obtained from a lot of hens and cocks.

In Western dishes, fish dishes are served absolutely free from bones. If a guest finds bones in the dish, it would be considered too horrible. In Chinese meals, fish is normally served whole and removing bones is regarded as part of the dining process.

UNIT 4

International Traveling

Learning Objectives

After learning this unit, you will be able to:
- analyze situations of international communication regarding traveling security, airport etiquette, means of transport and packing rules;
- learn and practice etiquette of international traveling and useful expressions;
- comprehend the definition of culture shock and ways to avoid it when traveling to a different cultural background.

Section I Warm-Up

1. Why do people travel? Listen to a song: "Traveling Light". After listening, come up with an imaginary story of the person portrayed in this song.
2. How much do you know about transport and traveling rules from your own experience?
3. Do you know how to pack before traveling? List the items you habitually take with you. Discuss with a partner, preferably someone of the opposite sex, compare your notes and explain the difference if there is any.
4. How can you guarantee your safety when traveling? List some tips that can help to keep you safe.

Section II Points to Remember

There are important points to remember and some rules to follow in present-day international communication. The following is a summary of the basics in regard to traveling security, airport etiquette, means of transport and packing rules. Referring to these points constantly may help you have a safer and more enjoyable travel.

Part 1 Traveling: Security

1. **What to Take Before You Travel**
   - Travel light.
   - Carry the minimum number of valuables.
   - Keep your passport, cash and credit cards locked in a safe hotel to avoid losing them.
   - Avoid handbags and outside pockets that are easy targets for thieves.
   - Keep medicines in their original, labeled containers.

2. **What to Leave Behind at Home**
   - Do not bring anything you would hate to lose.
   - Leave a copy of your itinerary with family or friends at home.

UNIT 4 International Traveling

- Make two photocopies of your passport identification page, airline tickets, driver's license and the credit cards that you plan to bring with you.

3. **Things to Arrange Before You Go**
   - Plan to stay in larger hotels with more security.
   - Book a room from the second to the seventh floors.
   - Get your house in order.
   - Find out if your personal property insurance covers you for loss or theft abroad.
   - Check on whether your health insurance covers you while you are abroad.

4. **Safety on the Street**
   - Be especially cautious in areas where you may be more easily attacked.
   - Try not to travel alone at night.
   - Avoid public demonstrations and other civil disturbances.
   - Keep a low profile and avoid loud conversations or arguments.
   - Do not discuss travel plans or other personal matters with strangers.
   - Beware of pickpockets.
   - Try to look purposeful when you move about.
   - Learn a few phrases in the local language.

5. **Safety in the Hotel**
   - Keep your hotel door locked at all times.
   - Meet visitors in the lobby.
   - Do not get on the elevator if there is a suspicious-looking person inside when you are alone.

6. **Safety on Public Transportation**
   - You should only take taxis clearly identified with official markings.
   - Do not accept food or drink from strangers.
   - Stay awake if possible.
   - Do not be afraid to alert authorities if you feel threatened in any way.

7. **Safety While Driving**
   - Keep car doors locked and wear seat belts at all times.
   - Avoid driving at night if possible.
   - Do not leave valuables in the car.
   - Do not park your car on the street overnight.

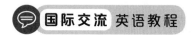

- Never pick up hitchhikers when traveling.
- Do not get out of the car if there is a suspicious-looking individual nearby.

8. **How to Handle Money Safely**
   - Deal only with authorized agents when you exchange money, buy airline tickets or purchase souvenirs.
   - If your possessions are lost or stolen, report the loss immediately to the local police.

9. **How to Take Medication Through Airport Security**
   - Label all medications clearly.
   - All medications are allowed through the airport security checkpoint, once they have been screened.

Part 2 Airport Etiquette

1. **Being Security Conscious**
   - Go through a series of security checks, before you can board your flight.
   - Answer security-related questions.

2. **Going Through Security Check Machine**
   - Remove particular garments before going through the security check machine.
   - Do so without questioning.

3. **Being Polite**
   - Remember that delays in any flight or travel plans are not caused by airport or airline crew.
   - Don't exhibit aggressive or threatening behavior.

4. **What to Do If You Miss Your Flight**
   - Do not lose your temper and start to blame the airport staff for their negligence.
   - Inclement weather and mechanical faults are two common reasons for missed flights. Calmly and politely ask for alternative arrangements.

Part 3 Various Means of Transport

1. **Air Transport**
   - When selecting a flight, remember that a flight that departs earlier in the day is

less likely to be significantly delayed than a later flight.
- Consider the potential adverse weather when choosing a transit city.

2. Rail Transport

    Advantages:
    - It pollutes less and rarely suffers from weather delays. You can talk to your companions, read a book, or have a snooze. You might have a meal in the dining car, make friends in the bar or watch a movie.
    - It is often easier to take care of small children on a train than on a plane or car.
    - Some people go by train solely for the amazing views on route, or to relish the extra time it takes, giving them time alone.
    - Traveling overnight is also a good way to save money on hostel or hotel accommodation.

    Disadvantages:
    - Trains are not the fastest way to travel and timekeeping cannot always be relied on.
    - In smaller countries, trains might only run once every few days and may not stop directly where you want to go.

3. Road Transport
    - The cost of road transport is relatively small.
    - The relative speed of vehicles is high (the major constraint is the government-imposed speed limits).
    - With a road network, route choice becomes very flexible.
    - Road transport has the unique opportunity of providing door-to-door service for both passengers and freight.

4. Water Transport

    Advantages:
    - It is the cheapest traffic means, and it plays an important role in international trade.
    - It possesses high load carrying capacity, and it requires lower motor power than airplanes.
    - It does not require any special infrastructure like roads or airports, and it brings many countries together.

Disadvantages:

- It is slow in speed and has a greater chance of being attacked while sailing on water.
- It can only be used when sufficient water is available. In the deep sea, if the boat is caught in a storm, it becomes difficult to rescue.
- Special maintenance is required to keep a boat water-tight.

Part 4 Packing Rules

1. **Making a Packing Plan**
   - Plan the contents of your suitcase by creating a packing list.
   - Crosscheck this packing list to determine if one item can cover multiple occasions.
   - Dark clothing, such as a black dress or blue jacket, can get you through most dinners and plays.
   - Check with your travel agent about the hotel's in-room amenities so that you will know what to leave behind.
   - Keep your makeup to a minimum to save space.
   - For each item you intend to bring, visualize how to make it smaller.
   - Once your travel kit is complete, be sure to pack it in your carry-on bag to avoid making a mess in your checked luggage and have it with you during the flight.

2. **The Art of Packing**
   - Iron everything before placing it in the suitcase.
   - Learn to fold.
   - T-shirts, jeans, skirts and sports coats can be rolled up and strategically positioned in a travel pack.
   - Pack tightly.
   - Carry travel documents, medication, jewelry, traveler's checks, keys and other valuables in your carry-on luggage.
   - Label each piece of luggage, both inside and out, with your name and telephone number, but not your home address.

UNIT 4 International Traveling

Part 5 Essentials for a Chinese

How to Overcome Culture Shock in a Foreign Country

It is common to experience culture shock when living in a foreign country for an extended period of time. Culture shock is defined as the feeling of disorientation, insecurity, and anxiety one may feel in unfamiliar surroundings. Values, behaviors, and social customs you routinely take for granted may no longer serve you in your new environment. By adapting to a foreign culture, you can overcome your culture shock and develop meaningful relationships with those around you, rather than feel anxious and confused in your new space.

- Keep an open mind: Do not automatically perceive anything that is different to be "wrong". Be an objective observer and facilitate the process of cross-cultural understanding. Do some background information research. Keep an open mind and find the reason for something you may not understand.

- Make an effort to learn the local language: Increase your communication skills. Integrate with the local community. Demonstrate your interest in the new country.

- Get acquainted with the social conduct of your new environment: Do not assume or interpret behavior from your own cultural perspective or "filter". Remember: If in doubt, check it out!

- Do not take cultural familiarity or knowledge at face value: Be careful not to attribute what you now believe you know to an explanation or rationale.

- Make sure you get to know people in your new environment: Respectfully ask questions, read newspapers, and attend a variety of festivals and events.

- Try to achieve a sense of stability in your life: Establish a routine. Foster a feeling of security.

- Maintain a sense of humor: Don't be too hard on yourself if you make a cultural gaffe or don't know what to do in a social situation. Laugh at yourself and others will laugh with you. Make an effort to understand their culture.

Section III Let's Do It!

Activity 1 Understanding Traffic Signs

When traveling, it is convenient and helpful to know some traffic signs. Look at the following signs, discuss them with your partner, and try to figure out what each sign symbolizes.

UNIT 4 International Traveling

Activity 2 Do You Like Traveling?

Make a short presentation about the topic "Do You Like Traveling?" Your presentation should include the following aspects:
- When do you like to travel?
- Who do you prefer to travel with?
- Where to travel?
- Why do you like to travel? (Give at least two reasons.)

Activity 3 Traveling Alone or with Others?

Introduction, elucidation of the theme, change of approach and summing up are the four steps in the composition of an essay; put in another way, they are opening, developing, changing and concluding. While comparing the two options, we can also take another approach—reversing as the third step.

Write a short essay on the topic "Taveling Alone or with Others". Remember to follow the format of opening, developing, reversing, changing and concluding.

_____
_____
_____
_____
_____

Activity 4 Favorite Means of Transportation

Describe your favorite means of transportation. You can use the following cue card as a reference.

Student's Cue Card:

> You should include:
> - What is it?
> - When and how often do you use it?
> - Why do you use it?
> - Why is it your favorite means of transportation?

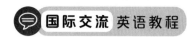

Activity 5　Role-Playing on Traveling Situations

Choose one of the following topics and role-play on it. Remember to switch roles with your partner.

- Booking a room
- Confirming flight reservation
- Checking in at the airport
- Going through security check

Activity 6　Predicting the Future Transportation

Discuss in a group what the future transportation would be like. Pool your ideas together. One member of each group will be the group representative and present in front of the class.

Section IV　Tool Box

1. Useful Words and Expressions

    1) Ticket Booking

    - 国内班机 domestic flight
    - 国际班机 international flight
    - 经济舱 economy class
    - 商务客舱 business class
    - 头等舱 first class
    - 班机号码 flight number
    - 单程机票 one-way ticket
    - 来回机票 round-trip ticket

    2) At the Customs

    - 护照检查 passport inspection
    - 商务签证 business visa
    - 观光签证 tourist visa
    - 延期 extend/prolong
    - 过境 stop over

UNIT 4 International Traveling

- 商品检查 commodity inspection
- 违禁品 contraband (goods)
- 验关 customs inspection
- 海关申报处 customs service area
- 免税商品 duty-free item
- 应纳税商品 goods subject to duty, dutiable goods
- 货币申报 currency declaration
- 入境登记卡 entrance registration card
- 入境签证 entry visa
- 出境登记卡 departure card
- 出境记录卡 disembarkation card
- 出境申请表，入境记录卡 embarkation card
- 出境检查 emigration control
- 出境签证 exit visa
- 安检 security check
- 预防接种证书 vaccination certificate
- 健康证明书 health certificate

3) At the Airport
  - 入境旅客休息室，入境大厅 arrival lounge/lobby
  - 入境手续 arrival procedure
  - 出境大厅，候机大厅 departure lounge/lobby
  - 直飞 direct flight
  - 转机 transfer
  - 候机大厅 terminal building
  - 转机询问处 tourist information office / transit information office
  - 转港休息室 transit lounge
  - 免税店 duty-free shop
  - 乘机手续台，旅客登机报到处 check-in counter
  - 登机证 boarding card
  - 补票处 fare-adjustment office
  - 登机门号码 gate number
  - 问讯处 information desk
  - 机场税 airport tax

4) On the Plane
- 机内免税销售 in-flight sales
- 盥洗室 lavatory
- 使用中 occupied
- 无人 vacant

5) Luggage Claiming
- 行李 baggage/luggage
- 随身行李 carry-on baggage
- 行李推车 luggage cart
- 行李申报单 baggage declaration
- 行李过磅处 baggage check-in counter
- 托运的行李 checked baggage
- 行李牌 baggage tag
- 行李领取处 baggage claim area

2. Useful Sentences

1) Ticket Booking
- I'd like to make a reservation for a flight to New York on September 15th.
- How much is airfare?
- I'd like to reconfirm my plane reservation, please.

2) At the Customs
- May I see your passport, please?
- How long are you going to stay in America?
- I will stay for one week.
- What is the purpose of your visit?
- I'm here for sightseeing.
- I'm only transiting this country.
- Do you have anything to declare?
- I have nothing to declare.
- This is a gift I'm taking to France.
- These are gifts for my friends.
- These are for my personal use.
- Do I pay duty on this?

UNIT 4 International Traveling

- What's the limit on duty-free liquor and tobacco?

3) At the Airport
    - What time do you start check-in?
    - Where do/may I check in for United Flight 706?
    - What time will boarding begin/start?
    - I'm connecting with AF (Air France) Flight 123.
    - Where can I get information on a connecting flight?
    - Is there an airport bus to the city?

4) On the Plane
    - Where is the lavatory?
    - Do you have Chinese newspaper?
    - I feel cold. May I have a blanket?

5) Luggage Claiming
    - Excuse me, where is the baggage claim area?
    - Where do I pick up my baggage?
    - Where can I get a luggage cart?
    - Where is the lost luggage office?
    - I can't find my baggage.
    - Here's my claim check.
    - Could you please check on it right now?
    - We may have lost some bags so we'd like to fill in a lost luggage report.
    - Please deliver my bag to my hotel as soon as you have located it.

Section V Do You Know?

Supplementary Readings

Read the following three passages and find out more about traveling. The answers to the questions at the beginning of each passage can be found through reading.

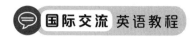

Passage 1 Harbin

> **Questions:**
> - In which aspects is Harbin introduced in this passage?
> - Why is Harbin an ideal place for raising cattle, cultivating corn, and instrument manufacturing?
> - Does Harbin have a perfectly comprehensive higher education structure? Why?
> - In what way can we say Harbin has unique conditions for developing cloud computing and establishing digital data centers?
> - After reading the passage, how would you summarize the features of Harbin in less than 200 words?

You are witness to a city of legends. At the northernmost point, and the easternmost end of China, it wakes at dawn each morning, and loses itself in ecstasy each night.

Across the street, the old and the young observe each other, with youthful passion on one side and meditative reflection on the other. The city integrates cultural diversities, breaks down geographical barriers, and is a harbor of bigger dreams, stronger personalities and clearer directions that transcend time and space.

Harbin's ancient origins are shrouded in the mists of time, but the city was propelled into the limelight a hundred years ago. There has never been a city so "Chinese" as Harbin, yet so exotic. Despite a century has gone by, Harbin is still full of vitality, excitement, stimulation and contradiction, and it is filled with a sense of Déjà Vu combined with greater uniqueness than any other city you have visited.

Child of Nature

Unlike cities that remain the same throughout the year, Harbin has four distinct seasons. Located at 45 degrees north latitude, the city provides ideal conditions for cattle raising, corn cultivation, and instrument manufacturing, earning it the reputation of the golden milk and corn belt.

The river blesses the city, brings the city spirit and brings the city life. Harbin grew up at the Songhua River, always in the spirit of bringing prosperity to both banks of the river.

Because people depend on it, the ecology of the Songhua River must be continuously improved to protect the mother river of the city and provide business opportunities to future generations, even if they are not yet visible. Environmental protection is not only a goal of economic development, but also part of this city's tradition.

East Meets West

Familiar strangers, foreigners who just arrived in Harbin will re-understand the meaning of this phrase in their heart. Over a short hundred years, from its peak when Harbin was home to people from 40 different nations, a Western architectural tradition has developed in the city. As a former financial and trade center of the Far East, a feeling for business has been passed down in Harbin's beloved. Like a city of heaven, youthful Harbin fosters a curious and tolerant atmosphere, regardless of race, language, culture or food. Nothing can stop its progress. With such striking uniqueness, it is like entering another universe; because of this, you will be gently joined to linger, passing through faces of familiarity, but always returning to discover something marvelous and new.

Ice City & Summer Capital

Interest in snow and ice sports is developing fast in China, which brings the ice city a huge number of enthusiasts and massive business opportunities from all over the world. The Ice and Snow Art Festival is already famous, spurring the city to offer ever more novelties to dazzle the visitors' eyes. Yabuli is not only the finest skiing competition place and tourist resort in China; it also boasts a year-round conference center for Chinese entrepreneurs.

Because the passion brought by the cold air of winter is not enough to satisfy the city, Harbin is reinventing itself as a resort with a different trademark—the summer capital. Harbin has many summer activities, making it Asia's newest hotspot for international conferences and grand expos. Harbin attracts a vast number of leisure tourists from around the globe, almost equivalent to the population of Beijing and Shanghai combined; this is why Harbin is regarded by many businesses as an important city to promote themselves. It is not for nothing that Harbin is ranked China's number one tourist destination by Chinese netizens.

City of Wisdom

In 1920, the shining rails of central eastern railway almost instantaneously brought modern Western engineering and scientific ideas into Harbin, and the establishment of Harbin Institute of Technology made the city a pioneer in modern scientific education. The PLA Military Institute of Engineering and other universities have also nurtured outstanding talents for Chinese industrialization and the country's epoch-making development miracle. Harbin has a perfectly comprehensive higher education structure, boasting the highest number of central government research institutes and key labs in the country; Harbin is a leading city in scientific education. The three power giants and the vehicle and pharmaceutical industries have trained many outstanding technical personnel. The steel industry is like the bones of the city and black gold is like the blood. Harbin has accumulated over the past hundred years a rich reserve of practical human resources, providing a steady stream of talents for enterprises to help them grow.

Top of China

Harbin, the northernmost provincial capital of China, situated at the center of Northeast Asia, has always been the prime city for trade with Russia, and the bridgehead for Sino-Russian trade and international trade in Northeast Asia. It is now building trade service platforms with vast development prospects. The rapid growth of high-speed road constructions, coupled with the early development and improvement of the railroad network, has given Harbin distinctive advantages in both domestic and foreign trade.

But a even more promising future awaits in the sky. With China's closest airport to North America, which is at an almost equivalent distance to North America, Europe and Southeast Asia, Harbin is the undisputed shipping hub in Northeast Asia. Harbin is now building an international air cargo hub, connecting North America and covering Northeast Asia, thus providing a powerful structural support for the development of higher manufacturing industry through modern logistics.

With stable geological structure, relatively low average temperature, abundant power provision and rich talent pool, Harbin has unique conditions for developing cloud computing and establishing digital data centers.

The World's Granary

The most dazzling thing can be both the most mundane and also the most glorious—the black earth. For centuries, all the stories in northeast China began and ended with this black earth where you could grow anything you wished for. China's most fundamental granary commodities are produced here, and the country's biggest producing areas for grains and milk are located here; and here, many famous global dairy brands find a green and safe supply of raw materials. In recent years, many food enterprises have invested in Harbin and achieved tremendous success, and the great northern granary with a grain production capacity of over 500 million kilograms still has the largest raw materials supply capacity. Meanwhile, Harbin is also contemplating how to provide better structural support to help enterprises to settle down, such as accelerating the construction of quality supply chains, and the recent world food expo will inject new vitality into the development of Harbin's food industry. Relying on the rich and fertile black soil, the status as a logistics center, forests and rivers, Harbin will continue to make the food industry a fresh catalyst to lead the city's development.

It is the northernmost part of China, but not the farthest; It is the coldest in China, but also the warmest. The three power giants once led the city's massive industrialization, but now international giants, such as Nestle, Danone, U.F. Union International Food, Ericsson, Toyota, Mitsubishi, Airbus and John Deere are reinvigorating Harbin like a fresh ocean breeze.

Along with the implementation of the new strategy, many new ideas of modern economic development have gradually taken shape. Harbin is committed to providing investors with all manners of possibilities, fresh inspiration, and more liberal market conditions, and has already become a blue ocean.

Passage 2 Digital Dunhuang

> Questions:
> ♦ Would you prefer this kind of digital or virtual traveling experience? Why or why not?
> ♦ What is the significance of the project of "Digital Dunhuang"?
> ♦ What's the purpose of the project of "Digital Dunhuang"?
> ♦ What has been done to make this project available?

Digital Dunhuang, an online resource database, became available in English from Sept. 20, 2017, marking a giant leap towards global sharing of the stunning Dunhuang resources.

More than 120 scholars and artists from Britain, France, Italy, the United States, South Korea, Japan, Brazil, as well as China attended the launch ceremony, after which they also discussed the Dunhuang School of painting, and its heritage and innovation.

The Dunhuang Caves, inscribed in the UNESCO World Heritage List, are a treasure house of ancient Chinese civilization.

The goal of Digital Dunhuang is to pool massive amounts of data related to the Dunhuang Caves—famous for the grottoes with ancient wall paintings—that have already been available or will be in the near future, including images, videos, and archaeological and protection materials.

Based on more than 20 years of arduous work in digitalizing the artworks, Digital Dunhuang is a large and integrated digital resource and service platform for

Dunhuang wall paintings and research results.

Stored in a structured and orderly way, these resources are permanently preserved for sharing with scholars and the public around the world. This is another effort to inherit and promote the splendid ancient Chinese civilization.

The Dunhuang Academy has so far completed digitalizing wall paintings of 150 caves and accumulated more than 300 TB of data. The amount will continue to increase as the work continues. Dunhuang documents and related research are also abundant. A great quantity of documents scattered around the world also need to be linked or included in Digital Dunhuang.

The Chinese version of Digital Dunhuang was launched on May 1, 2016. It provides high-resolution digital resources and virtual tours of 30 Dunhuang Caves in the Northern Wei Dynasty (386–534), Western Wei Dynasty (535–556), Northern Zhou Dynasty (557–581), Sui Dynasty (581–618), Tang Dynasty (618–907), Five Dynasties (907–960), and Yuan (1271–1368) Dynasty.

Passage 3 The Politics of Travel

> Read the questions first, and then find out whether the statements are true or false while reading the passage.
> ♦ Tourism threatens the environment. (   )
> ♦ Taking a shower in the Himalayas can lead to global warming. (   )
> ♦ Taking an airplane contributes to climate change. (   )
> ♦ There is no good side to tourism. (   )
> ♦ Tourism changes tradition. (   )
> ♦ Working holidays will not help the environment. (   )

Tourism has seriously damaged fragile ecosystems like the Alps, the winter skiing playground of Europe, and the trekking areas of the Himalayas. Worldwide, it poses a serious threat to coastal habitats like dunes, mangrove forests and coral reefs.

It fuels a booming and usually illegal trade in the products of threatened wildlife, from tortoise shell and coral to ivory. Its "consumers" inevitably bring their habits and expectations with them—whether it's hot showers and flush toilets or well-watered greens for golfers. In the Himalayas, showers for trekkers often mean firewood, which means deforestation. In Hawaii and Barbados, it was found that each tourist used between six and ten times as much water and electricity as a local. In Goa, villagers that were forced to walk to wells for their water had to watch as a pipeline leading to a new luxury hotel was built through their land. Over the past decade, because of its appetite for land, water and herbicides, golf has emerged as one of the biggest culprits, so much so that "golf wars" have broken out in parts of Southeast Asia; campaigners in Japan, one of the chief exponents of golf tourism, have launched an annual World No Golf Day.

This is not to say tourism can't do some good—but the cost-benefit equation is complex. Historic monuments, houses and gardens thrive on visitors. In most parts of the world, notably in southern and eastern Africa, tourism underpins the survival of wildlife. Why else would small farmers put up with elephants trampling over their crops? Whale watching is now a bigger business than whaling. In the uplands of Rwanda, known to millions through the film *Gorillas in the Mist*, the mountain gorilla's salvation lies partly in the income and interest generated by tourists visiting in small groups. In Kenya, a lion's worth is estimated at $7,000 a year in tourist income—for an elephant herd the figure is $610,000. And if wide ranges of large animals are protected, then so are their habitats—the national parks.

Yet none of these gains are unqualified. To see whales and gorillas, for example, you have to travel by car, coach or plane. Each time you do so, you're actually setting fire to a small reservoir of gasoline and releasing several roomfuls of carbon dioxide into the atmosphere. Transport is the world's fastest-growing source of carbon dioxide emissions; leisure travel accounts for half of all transport. The cumulative result of such activity is one of the biggest disruptions in the Earth's history—global warming, climate change and rising seas.

Some observers now argue that tourism can strengthen local cultures by encouraging an awareness of tradition and the ceremonies and festivals that go with it. But what's the value of tradition if it's kept alive self-consciously, for profit, and bears little relation to real life—which, today, across the world, grows ever more uniform? The pressures of tourism breed a phenomenon often referred to as "Disneyfication", in which culture and history are transformed, and the authentic giving way to Disney-like replicas. What's undeniable is that tourism, in one way or another, changes tradition.

In truth, there are no easy answers to the dilemmas posed by mass tourism. Awareness, certainly, is a step forward—the knowledge of what it means to be a tourist. With that comes the ability to make better choices, where and how and even whether to travel. An increasing number of non-profit organizations offer working holidays, in which the economic and social asymmetries that lie at the heart of the holiday industry are somewhat redressed: The tourist takes but also gives. Among the best-known is the environmental research organization Earthwatch.

Such initiatives are undoubtedly one of the ways forward for tourism. The world, clearly, is not going to stop taking holidays—but equally clearly we can no longer afford to ignore the consequences. And if one of the major culprits has been the industrialization of travel, a genuinely postindustrial tourism, with the emphasis on people and places rather than products and profits, could turn out to be significantly more planet-friendly.

UNIT 5

Accommodation

Learning Objectives

After learning this unit, you will be able to:

- understand different types of accommodation;
- analyze situations of international communication regarding check-in, room service, check-out in a hotel and renting a flat;
- compare the differences between living in a dormitory and living at home;
- learn about how to book a hotel room.

Section I Warm-Up

1. Look at the following pictures. What types of accommodation are they?

1) _____

2) _____

3) _____

4) _____

2. What other types of accommodation can you think of? Write them down.

_____
_____
_____
_____

Section II Points to Remember

There are important points to remember and some rules to follow in present-day international communication. The following is a summary of the basics in regard to the types of accommodation, hotel booking, check-in, hotel service and check-out, tips for living in a hotel, and how to rent a flat. Referring to these points constantly may help you live conveniently and safely abroad.

Part 1 The Definition and Types of Accommodation

1. **The Definition of Accommodation**
   - Accommodation is a dwelling or place of temporary residence. It is a place to live in, such as a room, flat, house, etc., or a place, such as a hotel, where food and shelter are provided, especially in American English.

2. **The Types of Accommodation**
   - Hotels.
   - Motels.
   - Hostels.
   - Homestays.
   - Flats/Apartments.

Part 2 Hotel Booking

- Decide what kind of hotel you want: economy, mid-price, chain, luxury, three-star, four-star, or five-star, and the location of the hotel before making reservations.
- Begin searching online travel agent sites to find prices for reservations.
- Cancel your reservation before the time limit according to the hotel policy, if you want to cancel your hotel booking after confirmation.

Part 3 Check-in, Hotel Service and Check-out

- When checking in at a hotel, make sure you have all necessary documents, such as your passport or hotel voucher.
- Be respectful of the hotel's rules and regulations, such as keeping quiet and complying with housekeeping schedules.
- Check with the hotel if room service is available beforehand and, if so, what services are included in the fee.
- Determine the check-out time and make sure you have everything ready beforehand, such as your room key, payment method, and additional documents required by the hotel.

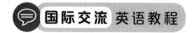

- Make sure all charges are settled.
- Keep the hotel room clean and tidy, and don't leave any personal belongings behind.

Part 4 Tips for Living in a Hotel

- When you're looking for a hotel, aim for a street with convenient transportation. Affluent residential areas tend to have more reliable transportation and fewer street threats.
- Besides valuables deposited in the hotel, be sure to bring the following things with you: cash, credit card, visa, ID card, camera, etc.
- When you enter your hotel room, make sure the door is securely closed and the deadbolt is working. Keep the deadbolt and safety bar on at all time.
- Be careful with the key to the hotel room. Don't lose it.
- Do not take things like perfume or wine in the hotel room for granted, usually they are not free.
- When selecting a hotel room, you need to maximize safety and security. Select a room between the 4th and 6th floors, and try to avoid rooms above the 6th floor, as this is the maximum height that fire ladder can reach.
- The "please make up this room" sign tells everyone you're not there. It's better to call room service while you're in your room.
- Conversely, the "do not disturb" sign can make the room seem occupied.
- Put expensive clothing on hangers under other garments. Robbers usually "shop" what they can see.

Part 5 How to Rent a Flat

- First, you need to search by exploring the Internet and compare prices, or look for an agency that specializes in renting flats.
- Then, you can visit the landlord to check the information.
- The monthly costs you need to pay are not just your rent. Unless these are included, you will need to pay for gas, electricity, water, broadband, and digital TV on top of your rent.

- Ensure that you are aware of your rights and responsibilities.
- Check the small print of your contract, including the duration of the tenancy, and what bills you're responsible for.

Part 6　Essentials for a Chinese

- Make sure you know the room service hours.
- Keep the door closed when the delivery person is outside your room.
- Don't tip the delivery person unless it is a special occasion or the service is exceptional.
- Keep the receipts in case of any additional charges that may be incurred.
- If you need to cancel or reschedule your room service order, do so promptly to avoid any fees or delays.
- Be respectful to the hotel staff and their time as they are working hard to ensure your stay is comfortable and enjoyable.

And you can add more...

Section III　Let's Do It!

Activity 1　Choosing the Accommodation

1. If you study abroad, what kind of accommodation will you choose? Why? Discuss with your partner. You can read the passage "The Types of Student Accommodation at the University of Manchester" on Pages 97–99 for your reference.
2. Introduce your dormitory life to your partner and compare differences between living in a dormitory and living at home. You may talk about the following points.
   - Your living environment.
   - Roommates.
   - Differences between living in a dormitory and living at home.
   - The pros and cons of dormitory life.

Activity 2 Booking a Hotel

1. Read the passage "How to Find and Book a Hotel Room" on Pages 99–103 and write a summary of the passage.

How to Find and Book a Hotel Room

___

2. Prepare a three-minute speech entitled "How to Book a Hotel Room". Present your speech in a small group of 4–5 people. The best in the group should go to the front and make the speech to the class. You can write down the keywords or the outline of your speech in the space below.

How to Book a Hotel Room

Beginning:

___

Body:

___

Ending:

___

UNIT 5 Accommodation

Activity 3 Check-in, Room Service and Check-out

Role-play the following dialogs in English based on the information given in Chinese.

1. Check-in

   (R: Receptionist   G: Guest)
   R: 您好。您预定房间了吗?
   G: 是的。我叫李华。
   R: 请稍等，我查一下。找到了。您定了一个双人房，住三天两夜，对吗?
   G: 是的。
   R: 请出示一下您的护照，然后填这个住房登记卡。
   G: 请问一下，退房时间是几点?
   R: 中午十二点。您的房间号是 502。这是您的房间钥匙和早餐券。服务生会帮您搬行李，把您带到房间。
   G: 谢谢。顺便问一下，餐厅在什么地方?
   R: 在二楼。这是有关我们旅馆信息的宣传小册子。希望您玩得愉快。

2. Room Service

   (M: Maid   G: Guest)
   M: 您好。请问有事吗?
   G: 我有些衣服要洗，应该交给您吗?
   M: 不是的，先生。我们旅馆有专门的洗衣服务。请把您的衣服留在房间里然后填这张卡。
   G: 我需要把衣服放在外面吗?
   M: 不必，就留在房里，打电话叫洗衣服务就会有人来取。
   G: 什么时候能洗好呢?
   M: 明天早上。
   G: 但是我今天晚上 8 点就要穿。
   M: 那您看看房间里有个盒子写着"快件"，把衣服放在里面。您 5 点钟就可以取衣服。

G: 谢谢。
M: 没关系。

3. Check-out

(C: Cashier   G: Guest)

G: 您好！我准备离开。

C: 请交还您的钥匙。您房间里还有行李吗？

G: 没有了。

C: 请稍等，我在算您的账单，一共是 280 美元。

G: 账单总数好像不对，这项收费是什么？

C: 哦，是早餐。

G: 明白了。那这一项呢？

C: 那是客房服务。

G: 好的。

C: 您是刷卡吗？

G: 是的。

C: 好，在这儿签字。这是您的收据，谢谢惠顾！

G: 谢谢，再见。

C: 再见。

Activity 4   Renting a Flat

You would like to rent a flat abroad, so you telephone the landlord to check the information about the flat. Role-play with your partner. The following information is for your reference.

Address: House number: _____
          Located on _____ Street
Close to: Shops: _____ mins' walk
          Bus stop/Subway: _____ mins' walk
Rooms: _____ bedrooms _____ kitchens _____ bathrooms
Large garden: Yes/No
Furniture: Yes/No
Household appliances: Yes/No

UNIT 5 Accommodation

Rent: $ _____ per month
Bills: Included or not
Visit flat at _____ am/pm

Student A's Cue Card:

- You would like to rent a flat.
- You telephone the landlord to check the information about the flat.

Student B's Cue Card:

- You are the landlord of a flat.
- You answer the phone and introduce your flat to the caller.

Activity 5 Listening About Flat Sharing

Listen to the audio "The Pros and Cons of Flat Sharing" and answer the following questions.

1) Why do many people choose to share the place with strangers?
2) Which rooms are commonly shared in a flat?
3) What can you do if you need to borrow something and no one is around to ask?
4) How can flat-sharing help your career?
5) What do shared flats usually lack?

Section IV Tool Box

1. **Useful Words and Expressions**
    1) Check-in
        - 可用的，空着的 available
        - 客满 no vacancy
        - 预定 reserve
        - 取消 cancel
        - 推迟 postpone

- 餐券，优惠券 coupon
- 登记表 registration form
- 单人房 single room
- 双人房，双床房 double room / twin room
- 套房 suite
- 商务房 executive room
- 特大号床 king-size bed
- 大号床 queen-size bed
- 保证金 deposit
- 接待员 receptionist
- 服务费 service charge
- 折扣 discount
- 大厅 lobby
- 行李 baggage/luggage
- 手提箱 briefcase
- 背包 shoulder bag

2) Hotel Service
- 总台 information desk
- 服务生领班 bell captain
- 男服务生 bellboy/bellman
- 行李存放处 cloakroom
- 行李员 porter
- 门房 doorman
- 急件 express
- 维修工 handyman
- 洗衣服务 laundry service
- 客房女服务员 chambermaid
- 万能钥匙 master key
- 贵重物品保管处 safe-deposit
- 保险箱，安全库 safe-deposit box

3) Check-out
- 找钱 change

- 收据 receipt
- 结账 pay the bill
- 发票 invoice

2. Useful Sentences

1) Check-in

- I made a reservation by phone today.
- A week ago I booked a room online.
- In what name did you make your reservation?
- I have a room reserved in the name of James Hill.
- Let me look through our reservation list. Sorry, we don't have a record of your reservation.
- Would you please fill out this form?
- Please show me your passport.
- We provide the first-rate service while we charge reasonable prices.
- I'll ask the bellboy to take you to your room.
- What's my room number?
- I hope you'll have a happy stay here.
- I wish you a pleasant stay with us.

2) Room Service

- Hot water is available 24 hours a day.
- When would you like me to make up the room?
- How much do you charge for this service?
- In case you have any problem, please feel free to tell us.
- We provide our customers with a variety of services such as currency exchange, food and drink, laundry, and mail.
- For detailed information, you can refer to the service directory.
- I'm always at your service.

3) Check-out

- I'd like to check out now.
- I'm here to settle my account.
- All these amount to 3,000 yuan.
- The third entry is for the room service you ordered.

- Here is your change and receipt.
- Did you enjoy your hours at this hotel?
- Shall I send a porter to carry the bag for you?
- Your service is terrific. I'm quite satisfied.
- Thanks for being with us. Hope to see you again soon.

4) Renting a Flat
- Is it fully furnished?
- How many bedrooms are there?
- What size are the bedrooms?
- Is there a garden?
- When can I move in?
- What kind of apartment do you have?
- I'd like to rent a one-bedroom apartment.
- When do you say that there would be an apartment available again?
- How much is the monthly rent?
- Do you have any apartment available right now?
- How long is the lease going to be?
- Do I have to sign a twelve-month lease? / Do I have to sign for a one-year term?
- How many square feet is that studio?
- How big is that apartment?
- Does the apartment get much natural light? / Does the room receive much sunlight?

Section V Do You Know?

Supplementary Readings

Read the following two passages and find out more about accommodation. The answers to the questions at the beginning of each passage can be found through reading.

UNIT 5 Accommodation

Passage 1 The Types of Student Accommodation at the University of Manchester

> **Questions:**
> - Is the cost of meals in catered halls included in the residence fee?
> - What is the main difference between catered halls and self-catered halls?
> - What do bedrooms include?
> - Does the university provide accommodation for families with children?
> - Can all the couples find their accommodation in the university? Why?

The majority of students coming to university will be moving away from home for the first time, which, while exciting, can also be a daunting experience. Therefore, we strive to offer a variety of accommodation options to meet every individual's needs and wants.

1. Catered Halls

In catered halls, meals are served in communal dining halls for you to enjoy with fellow residents. Meals are served throughout the year, except for vacation times and bank holidays, and their cost is included in the residence fee, making budgeting easier. Varied and extensive menus are always offered, including vegetarian and vegan options, and provision can also be made for those with special dietary requirements. The majority of catered halls also have smaller kitchen facilities, allowing you to prepare meals at weekends or during the day.

Meals Provided

1) Breakfast

- Five dishes with toast
- Cereal, fruit and yoghurt bars
- Hot and cold beverages

2) Dinner

- Hot main dishes (vegan, vegetarian, fish & meat)

- Salad bar
- Dessert (warm dessert, fresh fruit salad, yoghurt or a piece of fruit)
- Hot and cold beverages

Where possible, we look to use the finest local products and the most ethical and sustainable suppliers.

In Fallowfield, catering is provided Monday to Friday, while in Victoria Park, it is served seven days a week, with Saturday and Sunday breakfast service being altered to brunch (approximately 11:30–12:30).

In both Fallowfield and Victoria Park breakfast is served from 7:30–9:30, and dinner on Monday to Friday is served from 17:15–19:15. In Victoria park dinner on Saturday and Sunday is served from 17:15–18:30.

2. Self-catered Halls

Self-catered halls offer flexibility and independence: You determine the food budget, prepare the meals and decide when and what to eat. Typically, those in self-catered halls are grouped in shared flats or corridors, where communal lounges and kitchens are provided. In each kitchen, you will find cupboards, cookers, microwaves, refrigerators and freezers. However, students are required to bring their own cutlery and crockery.

Accommodation Facilities

1) Bedrooms

Bedrooms include a bed, desk, chair, wardrobe and shelving, with washing facilities (shower, wash-basin, toilet, etc.) shared with fellow residents. The ratio of bathrooms to residents is typically 4:1, depending on the hall. This is the same for bedrooms with a basin. For more hall-specific information, please visit the relevant webpage.

2) Ensuite Facilities

In addition to the standard facilities, ensuite study bedrooms include an adjoining room with a shower cubicle, wash-basin and toilet.

3. Family Accommodation

The university does not provide accommodation for families with children but does have a very limited supply of accommodation for couples. As demand exceeds supply this type of accommodation cannot be guaranteed. Through the Manchester Student Homes, many families and students with partners can also find flats or houses in the private rented sector. Accommodation for couples is at Horniman House.

4. Provision for Special Requirements

Students also have the opportunity to choose "moderated lifestyle" halls. They can request to live in halls that have adapted a moderated/reserved lifestyle in respect of alcohol, parties, noise, etc. We do not envisage being able to guarantee a permanently quiet or alcohol-free environment, but by grouping like-minded people together, we hope to at least provide a suitable environment.

Passage 2   How to Find and Book a Hotel Room

> Predict whether the following statements are true or false. Then read the passage and check your answers.
> - If you have a limited budget, you will end up staying in a cheap hotel. (   )
> - If you are traveling as a family or in a big group, you might consider booking a suite with a separate living area and bedrooms. (   )
> - Online search engines always show extra surcharges or fees for rooms. (   )
> - Calling the hotel directly can get you a last-minute booking or a better rate. (   )
> - Many hotels advertise group rates online and can often offer better rates. (   )
> - You can confirm your hotel room reservation by printing out a receipt at the end of your online booking session. (   )

Finding a good hotel and making a reservation can be stressful, especially if you are trying to book a hotel room for a large family or at the last minute. With many hotel reservations done online, there are online tools you can use to compare rates before booking the right room for you and your family. If you have never booked a hotel room before, you can do it easily and quickly by following several simple steps.

1. Finding a Good Hotel

Step 1

Determine your budget. Before you look for a hotel and make a reservation, you need to ensure the hotel will meet your budget and your needs. You should first determine your budget, or how much you can spend, when booking a hotel room. This will help you narrow down your search and be efficient with the time you spend looking for a hotel and booking a room. Having a limited budget does not mean you will end up staying in a cheap, dirty hotel. In fact, there are many discount options available for visitors on a budget.

On the flip side, you may be traveling for work and have the ability to pay for your accommodation on the company's account. In this case, an affordable hotel rate may not be as much of a priority for you.

Step 2

Think about your required accommodations during your stay. Do you need enough room for a family of four, or do you just need enough room for yourself? Consider how big you would like the hotel room to be, including how many beds and bathrooms you need. If you are traveling with your family, you may need two queen beds and one large bathroom. If you are traveling alone, you may just need one queen bed and one decently sized bathroom.

If you require facilities for people with disabilities, call the hotel to confirm if they have wheelchair access or offer amenities for the disabled.

Consider whether or not you require extra amenities, such as a spa or a fitness center. If you need a stable Internet connection, look for hotels that include free Wi-Fi in their nightly rate.

If you are traveling as a family or in a big group, you might want to consider booking a suite with a separate living area and bedrooms so that the whole group can be accommodated without space and privacy constraints.

Step 3

Identify your ideal location or area. Sometimes, location can trump budget or accommodation requirements, especially if you are looking for a location that is convenient. Are you looking for a hotel that is close to a work event or conference, or a hotel that is close to a specific tourist attraction? You may decide to live somewhere downtown, which will allow you to access different parts of the city easily. Or, you may decide to choose a more secluded location so that you have some privacy and can drive or walk to and from the main areas of town.

If you are traveling on business, you may decide to search for hotels that are close to a work conference or meeting.

If you are traveling for pleasure, look for hotels that are within walking distance to a hot spot, or hotels that offer packages that include car rentals so that you can get around easily.

Step 4

Search for hotels online. The quickest way to look for hotels is to browse online through a hotel search engine. These search engines will allow you to specify your planned days of travel, how many nights you require, your ideal location, and the amenities you need, if any. You can also specify how much you are willing to spend on the hotel.

Once you enter this information into the search engine, you will be presented with several hotel options. You can sort by price from lowest to highest, or use the map option to see hotels that are closer to a certain area or location.

Keep in mind that online search engines don't always show extra surcharges or fees for rooms. Note any small print next to the room price before you consider it.

Step 5

Compare hotels using discount search tools. You can also use discount search tools to compare several hotel options at once. All you need to do is to specify your travel dates and your price range. These sites will then search multiple databases for you and present several hotel options that best match your needs with discounts or lower rates.

Read the reviews of the hotels you are considering to get an idea of cleanliness, customer service and amenities. Weigh the reviews against the price and location of the hotel to determine if it will meet your needs.

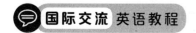

Some discount search tools require you to book the hotel room before knowing exactly which hotel you will be staying in. Always read the fine print before you book a room to ensure you won't be surprised by any restrictions or stipulations.

Step 6

Call the hotel to get a better rate. Calling the hotel directly can land you a last-minute booking or a better rate. You may also be able to get a better idea of the customer service offered at the hotel, as you will be able to speak to the front desk and ask them specific questions about the hotel. Try to call in the late evening, as mornings and afternoons are often busy for the front desk. You may want to ask questions such as:

- Is there a restaurant or bar on site? Is breakfast included in the nightly rate?
- Do you offer non-smoking rooms?
- Is the hotel near public transportation? Do you offer transportation like rental bikes?
- How far is the hotel from a specific location or area, such as the beach?
- Which side of the hotel has a better view or less noise?
- Is the area around the hotel safe?
- Are there facilities available for the disabled?
- What is the hotel's cancellation policy?

2. Booking the Hotel

Step 1

Reserve the room online. Once you have selected your hotel room, you can reserve it online through the hotel website. You will need to provide basic information about yourself for the booking, such as your full name and your travel dates.

If you are looking for a group rate for a conference or a wedding, call the hotel directly and speak to the front desk. Many hotels do not advertise group rates online and can often offer you better rates over the phone.

Step 2

Pay for the room with your credit card. Many online bookings will require payment via a credit card. If you are traveling on a business trip, you may use the company credit card to pay for the hotel.

Always check if your credit card company or AAA provider offers any discount on hotels so that you can use them when you pay for the room.

If you are staying at the hotel for an extended period of time, you may be able to pay for the first 2 to 3 nights upfront and then cover the rest of your stay once you get to the hotel. You will then be required to leave your credit card number on file and settle your bill at the front desk on your check-out day.

Step 3

Confirm the room is booked. You can confirm your booking by printing out a receipt at the end of your online booking session. You can also ask the hotel to send you a receipt as proof of payment if you book the hotel over the phone.

Step 4

Read over your receipt to confirm that everything is correct. This includes your travel dates and agreed-upon room rates. The hotel should specify all required fees and charges before you pay for the room or reserve the room. Extra fees, such as cleaning fees or parking fees, should be explained to you by the hotel so that you will not be surprised by any hidden fees when you check out.

UNIT 6

Applying for Universities Abroad

Learning Objectives

After learning this unit, you will be able to:
- understand basic procedures of applying for universities abroad;
- analyze situations of international communication regarding accepting and declining offers and visa application interviews;
- compare the differences between entering universities at home and applying for universities abroad;
- introduce how to apply for universities abroad;
- write a letter to accept or decline an offer.

Section I Warm-Up

1. Do you want to study abroad someday? Why or why not?

2. What are the advantages and disadvantages of studying abroad?

3. Could you list the basic procedures that you can think of for applying for universities abroad?

4. In your opinion, what is the toughest part of applying for foreign universities?

5. If you study abroad, what materials should you prepare?

Section II Points to Remember

There are important points to remember and some rules to follow in present-

UNIT 6 Applying for Universities Abroad

day international communication. The following is a summary of the basics about applying for universities abroad, accepting and declining offers, applying for passports and visas. Referring to these points constantly may help you apply for universities abroad more effectively and easily.

Part 1   Basic Steps of Applying for Universities Abroad

1. **Finding Your Desired Universities**

    You need to consider:
    - Number of students.
    - Academic programs.
    - Cost of study.
    - Ranking of the university and the major.

2. **Comparing Target Universities**
    - Objectives, methodology and approach of your chosen academic program.
    - Admission/Entrance requirements.
    - Availability of assistantships and funds in your chosen field.
    - Research facilities.
    - Location profile of students enrolled.

3. **Requesting for Application Forms**
    - Visit the university's website and search for the "admissions" or "application" section.
    - Look for a link to download application forms or find information about how to apply online.
    - If the university does not have an online application process, look for contact information for the admissions office.
    - Email or call the admissions office and ask if they are able to send you application forms by mail or email.
    - Provide them with your personal information, such as name, address, and date of birth, so they can send you the correct forms.
    - Follow any instructions provided by the admissions office regarding deadlines for submitting applications and required materials.

4. **Taking Various Required Tests**
   - Standardized tests, e.g., TOEFL, IELTS.

5. **Preparing for Application Paperwork**
   - Recommendation letters from professors or senior professionals.
   - Statement of Purpose (SOP).
   - Curriculum Vitae (CV).
   - Copies of academic transcript.
   - Proof of English proficiency.

6. **Completing and Sending Application Materials**
   - Send your application materials before the deadline.

7. **Making Preparations in the Admission Stage**
   - Learn about the program curriculum, length of program and optional courses.
   - Choose the best funding offer, or choose the best program considering the costs.
   - Calculate the cost of living.
   - Learn about the university's location and safety of the neighborhood.
   - Learn about the local climate, social life, available facilities, accommodation and housing.

Part 2　Accepting and Declining Offers

- Study letter templates for accepting and declining offers.
- Write to one university to confirm your acceptance of its offer.
- Write in due time to other universities to decline their offers politely.

Part 3　How to Apply for a Passport

- Provide the identification card.
- Prepare certificate of residence and passport photos.
- Go to the authorized institution, usually a police station, to fill out a passport application form.
- Submit the application form and supporting documents in person.
- Pick up your passport within 10 to 15 working days.

UNIT 6 Applying for Universities Abroad

Part 4 How to Apply for a Visa

1. How to Apply for a UK Visa
   - Step 1: Visit the UK Visas and Immigration website to apply for a visa online.
   - Step 2: To complete the application process, you must make an appointment and attend on time at one of the visa application centers in China.
   - Step 3: On the day of your appointment, bring your appointment letter and application pack, your passport and another form of valid identification.
   - Step 4: Register your fingerprints and photographs (known as biometric information collection) at the visa application center.
   - Step 5: Choose whether you would prefer to collect your documents in person at the visa application center or have them delivered to you by EMS.

2. How to Apply for a US Visa
   - Step 1: Select the visa type: studying in the US (F, M).
   - Step 2: Complete the DS-160 online application.
   - Step 3: Schedule your appointment through the appointment center and pay the application fee.
   - Step 4: Attend the interview at the chosen location.
   - Step 5: Go to the local CITIC bank to pick up your passport and visa (if approved).

Part 5 Essentials for a Chinese

The following are some rules to remember when you apply for universities abroad:
- Make sure your chosen university is a good match for your interests and personality.
- Look closely at the courses offered by the institutions you're considering and make sure they match your own interests and aims.
- Submit relevant documents before the deadline.
- Be punctual, polite and honest during the visa application interview.
- Get all your documents ready when applying for your passport or visa.
- Write a letter to the admission staff when you decide to decline the offer.

And you can add more...

Section III　Let's Do It!

Activity 1　Applying for a University in the UK

1. Prepare a three-minute speech entitled "How to Apply for a University in the UK". Present your speech in a small group of 4–5 people. The best in the group should go to the front and make a speech to the class. You can write down the keywords or outline of your speech in the space below.

How to Apply for a University in the UK

Beginning:
_____
_____
_____

Body:
_____
_____
_____

Ending:
_____
_____
_____

2. Discuss with your partner the differences between entering universities at home and applying for universities abroad, and write down your conclusion below.

_____
_____
_____

UNIT 6 Applying for Universities Abroad

Activity 2   Accepting and Declining Offers

If you have received the acceptance letter, a letter of intent and relevant notices, you should make a decision to accept or decline the offer. Study the following two letter templates and write your own letters.

1) Declining the Offer

> Dear (Name of the Admissions Director/Committee),
>
> After much deliberation, I wish to decline my offer of admission to (Name of Rejected University). I will be attending (Name of Accepted University) in Spring 2024. I appreciate the opportunity to attend (Name of Rejected University). Thank you for your time and consideration.
>
> Sincerely,
>
> (Student's Full Name)

Dear _____ ,

_____
_____
_____
_____
_____
_____
_____

Sincerely,

_____

2) Accepting the Offer

> Dear (Name of the Admissions Director/Committee),
>
> I am writing to notify you of my decision to accept your offer to enroll in the Clinical Psychology program at Graduate School. Thank you for your time and consideration. I look forward to attending your program this fall and am excited for the opportunities that await me.
>
> Sincerely,
>
> (Student's Full Name)

Dear _____,

_____
_____
_____
_____
_____

Sincerely,

_____

Activity 3　How to Apply for a Passport

1. Work in groups to brainstorm the documents you should prepare when you apply for a passport.
2. Discuss how to apply for a passport in groups. Students who have got their passports can talk about their application experience.
3. Surf online to find the visa-free countries for a Chinese passport and write them down.

Activity 4　How to Apply for a Visa

1. List the documents you should prepare if you apply for a visa to Canada.

2. If you go to the United States, you are required to attend a visa interview at the US Embassy or Consulate in the country where you live. The interview process will include digital fingerprinting and potentially require additional supplementary information. In the interview, the interviewer may ask questions in four main areas:
   - Is there anything fraudulent in the student's admission application or visa

UNIT 6 Applying for Universities Abroad

application?
- Is the student qualified to attend the institution that she/he is planning to go to?
- Are there sufficient funds to support the student's education without working in the destination country?
- Does the student intend to return to China after the program finishes?

What other questions may be asked in the interview? Discuss with your partner and write them down, then role-play the visa interview with your partner.

_____

_____

_____

_____

Activity 5 Learning About the Relationship Between Overseas Students and the Economy

Listen to the audio "Overseas Students Add £20bn to the UK Economy", and answer the following questions.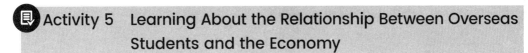

1) How many international students go to universities in the UK each year?
2) What do overseas students spend their money on according to the report?
3) What type of students does the Home Office say it will not limit?

Section IV Tool Box

1. **Useful Words and Expressions**
   1) Education
      - 学位 degree
      - 大专学位 college degree
      - 学士学位 bachelor's degree
      - 硕士学位 master's degree
      - 博士学位 doctoral degree
      - 毕业 graduation
      - 毕业证 graduation certificate

- 学位证 degree certificate/diploma
- 成绩单 transcript
- 中考 senior high school entrance examination
- 会考 secondary education examination
- 高考 college entrance examination
- 学分 credit
- 必修课 compulsory course
- 选修课 optional/elective course
- 平均成绩点数（学分绩）GPA (Grade-Point Average)
- 暑期学校 summer school / summer program
- 课外活动 extracurricular activity

2) Admission Application
- 录取工作人员 admission officer
- 升学顾问 counselor
- 截止日期 deadline
- 常规录取 regular admission
- 滚动录取 rolling admission
- 补充材料 supplemental information
- 录取通知 offer
- 延期 defer
- 拒绝 deny/reject

3) Visa Application
- 在读证明 studying certificate
- 工作收入证明 working certificate / employment certificate / income certificate
- 银行账单 bank statement
- 银行账户 bank account
- 户口本 household register
- 房产证 property ownership certificate
- 完税证明 tax clearance certificate
- 个人所得税单 personal income tax record
- 债券 bond
- 基金 fund
- 股票 stock

UNIT 6 Applying for Universities Abroad

- 租金收入 rental income
- 退休金 pension

2. Useful Sentences

1) Applying for Universities Abroad
    - My name is..., and I am from (City/Province/Country).
    - I am currently a (Grade Level) student studying in....
    - I have a strong interest in (Your Field of Study) and would like to pursue my further education in this field at your prestigious university.
    - The reason why I am applying for this program is that I believe it will provide me with the best opportunity to further develop my knowledge and skills in (Your Field of Study).
    - I am particularly attracted to your university because of its excellent reputation and renowned faculty members in (Your Field of Study).
    - I have always dreamed of studying abroad, and I believe that your university can offer me the best environment to achieve my academic goals.
    - I have consistently maintained a high academic record throughout my studies, achieving a GPA of ....
    - In addition to my academic achievements, I have also been actively involved in extracurricular activities such as ...
    - I have taken courses related to (Your Field of Study) and have gained valuable experience in (Your Skills or Achievements).
    - I believe that this major will provide me with the necessary skills and knowledge to succeed in my future career endeavors.
    - I am drawn to the challenges and opportunities that come with pursuing a degree in (Your Field of Study), and I am confident that I have the passion and dedication required to excel in this field.
    - As a hardworking and dedicated individual, I am committed to achieving my academic goals and making the most of my time at your university.
    - I possess strong problem-solving skills, effective communication abilities, and the ability to work well under pressure, which I believe are essential qualities for success in any field.
    - I am an adaptable and open-minded person who enjoys learning from diverse perspectives, and I believe that studying at your university will provide me

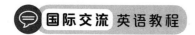

the opportunity to broaden my horizons and gain new insights into various cultures and ways of thinking.
- Thank you for considering my application.
- I look forward to the possibility of studying at your esteemed university and contributing to its academic community.
- If you require any additional information or documents, please do not hesitate to contact me.

2) Interview Questions of Visa Application
- Why do you want to study in the US?
- How many universities/schools have you applied for? / How many of them admitted you? / Why do you want to study in this university/school?
- How many of them give you financial aids?
- Do you know where this university/school is? Do you know where you will study in the US?
- How long will you study in the US?
- What will you study? / What do you want to study? / What's your major? / What's your subject?
- Why do you want to study Computer Science? / Why do you choose this major/subject?
- How about this university/school's tuition and fees?
- What are your parents' jobs? / What do your parents do?
- What do you plan to do in the future? What is your plan for the future?

Section V Do You Know?

Supplementary Readings

Read the following two passages and find out more about college applications. The answers to the questions at the beginning of each passage can be found through reading.

UNIT 6 Applying for Universities Abroad

Passage 1 How to Apply for a University in the UK

Read the questions first, and then find out whether the statements are true or false while reading the passage.

- If you care more about your university experience, you may place more emphasis on a school's ranking. (   )
- If you have already known what course you want to choose, this will help you determine which school you should apply for. (   )
- The best way for you to choose the right university is simply to visit the school and get a first-hand feel for the campus culture. (   )
- You'll need to pass an English language test if you're going to study in the UK from abroad and English isn't your native language. (   )
- If you live outside the UK, you'll need a student visa to enter the country. (   )
- You should write a personal statement explaining why you want to study in the university. (   )
- You should submit your application before the deadline. (   )

The United Kingdom (UK) is home to more than 150 universities, including some of the oldest and most prestigious schools in the world. However, in order to attend one of these universities, you need to go through an application process that can seem daunting to some people, especially if you don't live in the UK. Luckily, by making sure you meet the right admission requirements and submit the proper qualifications, you can take a lot of the stress out of applying for UK universities.

Choosing a University

Step 1

Make a list of what's most important to you in a university. There are over 150 universities in the United Kingdom that offer a variety of programmes and courses. In order to make it easier for you to choose the right university, rank those features of a university that are most important to you, from most important to least important.

For example, if your top priority is to graduate from a prestigious school, you might consider a university's ranking to be most important. If you care more about your university experience, you may place more emphasis on a school's location or campus life.

Consider what you want out of your experience at university. Some schools will offer appealing study abroad options, while others might offer you the chance to gain a year of experience in the industry you plan to work in.

Step 2

Look for schools that have strong departments in your desired course. If you have already known what course you want to study, this will significantly narrow your search and help you determine which university you should apply for. See which universities offer your course and how they compare to each other.

For example, if you want to study Burmese, you can only study at the University of London. However, if you want to study a more general subject like Chemistry, there are dozens of universities to choose from.

Step 3

Narrow your search by location if applicable. You may decide that what course you choose is less important than where you live. If this is the case, use location as a way of narrowing down your choice of potential universities.

For example, if you'd strongly prefer to live in a city instead of the countryside, consider universities in cities like London or Manchester.

If you'd like to live near the ocean, you might apply for schools like the University of Aberdeen, Bournemouth University, or Aberystwyth University.

Step 4

Visit the schools you're interested in if possible. You may find that the best way to choose the right university for you is to simply visit the school and get a first-hand feel for the campus culture. If you're able to travel to the UK, pay personal visits to 3 or 4 schools that you're seriously considering and see if they are a good fit for you.

While visiting the schools, talk to other students you meet. Ask them what it's like to live and study at the university, if there are other international students who attend the school, or if the university has any social clubs you might like to join.

Step 5

Choose universities in the UK by ranking if you can't visit them. Other than seeing them in person, perhaps the best way to judge British universities is by their national and international rankings. Search online for rankings of different schools in the UK and see which ones are consistently high in rank, as these are generally considered the top schools in the country.

For example, the University of Oxford, the University of Cambridge, and Imperial College London are commonly considered among the best universities in the UK, so they consistently ranked very high compared to other schools.

Meeting the Admission Requirements

Step 1

Check the required qualifications for the specific courses you're interested in. Many university courses have specific requirements that all incoming students must meet before enrolling. Because courses vary in their requirements, check each course provider's website to find out what qualifications they require.

For example, some courses will specify a certain degree (or equivalent level of education) that you must earn, as well as relevant language or research skills.

Note that these qualifications are stated in UK terms (e.g., A-level). If you're an international student, contact the course provider to find out how they determine equivalent qualifications from foreign countries.

Step 2

You'll need to pass an English language test if you're going to study in the UK from abroad and English isn't your native language. Note that you'll need to pass one English test to gain your entry visa and another more advanced English test to enroll in a university.

The UK Border Agency requires all visa applicants to have a basic working knowledge of English. This can be done by taking one of a variety of language tests. The complete list of applicable tests and minimum acceptable grades can be found on the British government's website.

UK universities usually list their English language requirements on their websites

as wall and will state the minimum acceptable grade for various language tests, including TOEFL, IELTS, and Cambridge English: Advanced.

Step 3

Obtain an entry visa if necessary. If you live outside the UK and are not a national of an European Economic Area nation, you'll need a student visa to enter the country. You can apply for a student visa from UK Visas and Immigration after you've been offered a spot in a particular course.

When applying for a visa, in addition to submitting the requested documents and information, you'll also need to prove that you can afford to live and study in the UK.

You don't need to obtain an entry visa to study in the UK if you are a Swiss national.

Step 4

Make sure you're able to afford tuition and fees. With a few exceptions, you will likely have to pay nearly £10,000 to attend university in the UK, although the cost of tuition varies from course to course. Check how much students from your home country will pay for the course you plan to study, and confirm you can afford it.

The most notable exception is for Scottish students and EU nationals studying in Scotland, who do not have to pay any tuition fees.

Completing and Submitting Your Application

Step 1

All college applications in the UK are submitted through the Universities and Colleges Admissions Service (UCAS). Thus, your first step should be to register with UCAS through their website and provide the requested details about yourself.

This is perhaps the simplest part of the application process, but make sure you don't incorrectly enter your personal information, as this may cause problems with your application down the line.

Step 2

Write a personal statement explaining why you want to study in the UK. Part of the application process involves writing a personal statement. If you're an international student, you'll need to specify why exactly you want to study in the UK, or, to put it another way, why you'd rather study in the UK than in your own country.

UNIT 6 Applying for Universities Abroad

For example, if you're aiming to study a more obscure subject like Burmese, you might state that the School of Oriental and African Studies at the University of London is arguably the best place to pursue this course outside of Myanmar. Similarly, if you want to study a more common subject that isn't well represented in your home country, you could emphasize that studying in the UK will give you opportunities you wouldn't otherwise have.

In your personal statement, you should also mention your English skills and any English language tests you have taken.

Step 3

Send the results of previous qualifications as required. UCAS is able to forward the results of certain international qualifications, but not all. If you're using the results of a degree program or exam in your home country to meet a course's qualifications, find out if you need to submit those results yourself.

For example, UCAS can submit your International Baccalaureate results on your behalf, but not most other results.

Other examples of international qualifications might include Advanced Placement (AP) Examination results, the Global Assessment Certificate, the Hong Kong Diploma of Secondary Education, and the Irish Leaving Certificate.

Step 4

Fill out and submit your application before the deadline. Different courses in the UK have different deadlines for submitting applications. Find out the deadline for your specific course and be sure to submit your application before the specified date.

For example, most courses in medicine require applications to be submitted in mid-October, while most other courses require you to submit the application until January.

From August 2018, there is an application fee of £13 if you're applying for just one course, or £24 for multiple courses and for late applications sent after 30 June.

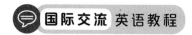

Passage 2 What You Should Know About Passports

> **Questions:**
> ♦ What is a passport?
> ♦ What does a passport contain?
> ♦ If your passport is lost, what should you do?

A passport is always required when traveling from one country to another. This is the authorized identification document issued by your country of citizenship that confirms your identity and nationality.

What Is a Passport?

It is a legal certificate issued by one's mother country to testify its owner's nationality and identity when crossing one country's frontier into another for travel, work and residence overseas. Actually the word "passport" in English means the pass of a port. In other words, it is the proof for a citizen to go through the international ports of all countries.

Function

For international travel across borders, a citizen must possess a legal passport which is issued by his/her own country's government, and simultaneously, a valid visa to the destination country is also often required.

If you have an accident during the period of travel or residence abroad, the host country should first confirm your status and nationality according to your passport, and then decide what to do next and how to handle it well. Similarly, the country issuing the passport and its embassy or consulate abroad must also decide how to provide assistance or diplomatic protection.

Types

At present, the passports issued by majority of countries in the world are generally divided into three types: diplomatic, service/official and regular ones. Some countries only issue one type (e.g., the UK); some countries only issue two of them (e.g., India, Pakistan, etc.); but there are also some countries that issue four or five types (e.g., the

UNIT 6 Applying for Universities Abroad

US, the France, etc.)

Content

As for content, all countries have similar requirements. They all have the national emblem, the country's full name and the type of passport printed on the cover, while the details of the passport use are usually printed on the back cover. The inside front cover is generally printed with the words requesting that the correlated military or administrative departments of the target country provide some necessary convenience and assistance to the passport holder.

Extension of expired passports is allowed in all countries, so passports have special pages for extension and remarks. In order to facilitate countries to issue visas, many additional blank pages are included within the passport, and each page is printed with the word "VISA" on it.

The texts printed on the passport are primarily in the native language of the issuer, but most countries also print the same texts in English.

Period of Validity

A passport is not a permanent credential, but a document with a limited period of validity. It is the legal proof during the period of validity only, which is also known as effective; otherwise it is invalid and is without legal status.

The period of validity in different countries is inconsistent and can be one, two, three and five years, or even ten years in some countries.

Generally speaking, countries require the passport to be valid for more than six months. If the period of validity is less than six months, you will have to apply for an extension or renewal.

Effective Area

The effective area is one of the important contents. In some countries, the passport is printed with words like "this passport is effective toward X (country name)" or "citizen who holds it is not allowed to go to X (country name) and X (area name)".

Make It Well-Kept

Before you apply for the visa for your destination country, you had better keep

your prepared passport well in a safe place at home. Do not always carry it with you. Once a visa is obtained, it is valid for entry into the destination country and holds a high value. Some international criminal groups and pickpockets specialize in stealing a passport and consider it more valuable than currency. They will trade it for money, or perform some other illegal activities using it as a shield. Therefore, you must keep yours under lock and key and be vigilant at all times, especially after you pass through the customs inspection and go on the oversea trip. You should always carry your passport along with you. Do not put it into your outside pockets or bags. It is much safer to put it into an inside pocket, which allows ready access for any situation you may encounter where your passport is required.

What to Do If It Is Lost

If you lose your passport before you go abroad, you should immediately report the loss to the security authorities and relevant issuing offices in your country, provide a detailed statement of the time and place of loss and state the basic information (name, gender, date of birth, number, etc.). If necessary, you may have to go to your local newspaper to report the loss (your name and number should be made public).

If it is lost abroad, you should rapidly report the case to the local public security organs and complete the detailed and essential registration procedure, simultaneously you should go to the nearest embassy or consulate as soon as possible to complete the loss registration, and then apply for replacement.

In order to prevent the loss, it is recommended that you'd better write the number on a jotter beforehand, or photocopy the whole content of its first page and then make it well preserved. All these preparations may offer you some convenient clues or good help in case you lose it.

Replacement

After you get a new passport, firstly you should carefully inspect it. If there is any doubt or error, you should immediately ask the relevant staff to apply for correction. If no problems or mistakes are discovered after your inspection, you can bring it back and keep it well.

Getting a passport is just the first step of the procedure for going abroad. Another necessary thing is that you should carry your passport and the correlated credential

UNIT 6 Applying for Universities Abroad

materials to go to the embassies or consulates of your target country to apply for a visa. When you obtain the visa, you should have an "International Prophylactic Inoculation Certificate". After purchasing the ticket to your target country and doing some pre-trip preparations, you can proceed with your journey abroad.

Before going abroad, you must have a passport with two consecutive blank pages, valid for at least six months from the date of submission of the visa application.

UNIT 7

Application Materials

Learning Objectives

After learning this unit, you will be able to:
- understand the principles of writing and submitting application materials;
- analyze situations of job application and school application in international communication;
- write a CV, a personal statement and reference materials in English;
- compare the cultural differences in application procedures between China and the West;
- comprehend the value of making your own application.

Section I Warm-Up

1. What is a CV? What is a resumé? Look up the two words in a dictionary and discuss the differences with your partner.

	Similarities	Differences
CV		
Resumé		

2. What is a PS? What is a SOP? Find out their full names in English and discuss the differences with your partner.

	Similarities	Differences
PS		
SOP		

3. Suppose you are applying for a part-time job in your school library. Write down any materials you can think of that you can use in the application process.

_____
_____
_____
_____
_____
_____

UNIT 7 Application Materials

Section II Points to Remember

There are important points to remember and some rules to follow in present-day international communication. The following is a summary of the basics in regard to application materials writing. Referring to these points constantly may help you write your application more effectively.

Part 1 Writing a CV/Resumé

Important Elements to Be Included in a CV/Resumé

1) Personal Information
   - Name.
   - Gender.
   - Date of birth.
   - Place of birth.
   - Ways of contact.

2) Educational Background
   - Schools you have attended.
   - Diplomas or certificates you have received.

3) Work Experience
   - Time and location of your previous work.
   - Roles, duties and achievements.

4) Special Traits
   - Skills.
   - Awards you have received.
   - Interests, uniqueness, etc.

5) Reference Materials
   - School transcripts.
   - Copies of certificates.
   - Copies of diplomas.
   - Reference letters.
   - Any proof to support your information given in the CV/resumé.

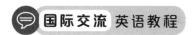

Part 2 Writing a Personal Statement or Statement of Purpose

Important Points to Remember When Writing a PS/SOP

- Be honest about your information.
- Choose the key points and highlights to describe.
- Pay attention to your grammar and vocabulary.
- Keep the length to 1–2 pages.
- The content should be unique, easy to read, and carefully selected to enable the readers to communicate with you while reading.
- There is no fixed format or template.
- Be original and creative.

Part 3 Preparing Recommendation Letters

1. **Points to Know When Getting Letters of Recommendation**
   - Letters of recommendation are from people who know you well.
   - There is no fixed format.
   - The style is formal.
   - The letter of recommendation should be printed with the name of the company or institution of the referee.

2. **Important Elements to Be Included in the Letter of Recommendation**
   - Who do you want to recommend?
   - How do you get to know this person, and for how long?
   - Why do you want to recommend this person?
   - What qualities does he/she have?
   - Your title and contact information.

Part 4 Preparing Reference Materials

1. **Points to Know When Preparing for Reference Materials**
   - Supporting materials for your application should be prepared.
   - Original or duplicates of all the materials ready for submission should be provided.

UNIT 7 Application Materials

2. **Typical Reference Materials**
   - Academic transcripts.
   - Certificates.
   - Diplomas.
   - Contact information of your referees.
   - Photos.
   - Posters.
   - Newspaper clips.
   - Journals.
   - Screenshots.
   - Anything that reflects your strengths and skills.

Part 5　Writing a Cover Letter

1. **Points to Know When Writing a Cover Letter**
   - It is intended for admissions officers or the recruiters.
   - It must be short.

2. **Important Elements to Be Included in a Cover Letter**
   - The source of information about this job vacancy.
   - The purpose of the cover letter.
   - Information about the job applicant.
   - Sound reasons for being a suitable candidate.
   - Contact information.

Part 6　Essentials for a Chinese

1. **Common Problems and Mistakes in Chinese Students' Application Materials**
   - Lack of content.
   - Lack of information.
   - Inappropriate addresses.
   - Misspellings.

- Mixed use of Chinese characters and English characters.

2. **Advice on the Writing of a CV/Resumé**
   - Don't exaggerate your experience or your activities.
   - Focus on your educational background.
   - Make sure that you include details of the courses and what you have learned from them.
   - Don't repeatedly point out your grades.
   - Supply supporting materials.

3. **Advice on the Writing of a PS/SOP**
   - Summarize yourself, your study, your ambitions, your future goals and career choices in 800–1,000 words.
   - Always try to be concise and say things in the briefest way.
   - Make sure that you don't make things sound exaggerated or better than they really are.
   - Just say what you need to say in an appropriate way.
   - Do not talk about your grades in your PS.
   - Focus on all aspects of you.
   - Remember to include your motivations for studying or working.
   - Try to show how you can contribute to the university or the company.

4. **Advice on Reference Letters or Letters of Recommendation**
   - Make sure that they are from professors or teachers who have taught you, and not from the dean of your college who does not know you well.
   - Make sure that you don't write the letters yourself.
   - Make sure that the letters are written by your teachers first and are in the original language, then translate them if necessary.
   - Try not to use templates.
   - Check spelling and grammar mistakes.

5. **Advice on the Writing of a Cover Letter or Email**
   - The proper length should be about half a page to one page of A4 paper.
   - Show more information about why you want to apply for that particular course or job in that university or company.

- Point out or highlight the key content of your application materials and get the reader interested to find out more information.
- Do not just talk about information in general.
- Do not write "Dear Sir", always write "Dear" with a name, and know who you are writing to.
- Try not to be too cold and informal, and show respect to the reader.

Section III Let's Do It!

Activity 1 Listening to Cover Letter Writing

Listen to the recording and fill in the blanks according to your understanding.

We are going to explain how to write a great cover letter for English speaking companies.

This is you. You want to apply for a position at the company of your dreams. You want to write a cover letter or (1)_____ and wonder how this is done in English speaking countries.

To make your cover letter stand out, you have to make (2)_____ count. Your letter of application should introduce you, show your personality, your (3)_____ and your enthusiasm! Studies have shown that managers hire people that fit the company culture best. The content should provide (4)_____ solid examples of your skills and experiences. But watch your English tenses! Use simple past for events finished (5)_____ and saying when exactly. For example, "I completed an internship two years ago". Use present perfect for events that started in the past but have not finished yet or are still (6)_____ for the present, for example, "I have completed a degree in media and I'm now looking for a job in this field."

Also, be sure not to undersell yourself, but also not to (7)_____. Be honest! Phrases like "I've never worked in advertising, but..." show what you haven't done. Rather, say what you have done and how it applies to (8)_____. HR managers read hundreds of applications every day. General, unspecific phrases that don't include the company impress no one! Rather, include (9)_____ facts about the company and your skills by saying, for example, "The business fields of the Dream Incorporation are a great chance to develop my previous experience in strategic management."

To make your cover letter effective, be as (10)_____ as possible. Vague and tired claims like "I have excellent interpersonal skills" may make the HR manager fall asleep too! Use action verbs, make yourself sound dynamic! What are these? Action verbs directly show off your skills and (11)_____. Good examples could be "I implemented...", "I prioritized...", "I stream-lined...", to name a few. These words will again help you avoid too long and (12)_____ phrases.

Ensure the letter is not longer than (13)_____, so make every word count.

Phrases like "As you can see from my CV" are unnecessary.

If there is enough time left, proof (14)_____ it the next day if you can.

Lastly, don't forget to check your letter for (15)_____ and make sure the layout is clean.

So, there you have it. When keep these points in mind, you will change your cover letter from boring and vague to sounding great and up to the point in a heartbeat. So don't waste time! Think of your dream company and start writing your personal cover letter now!

Activity 2 CV Editing

The following is a poorly written CV. Work in groups to improve it. You can add some of your information if necessary.

> Gilbert Zhang
> Home address: B10 123 HIT (the second campus)
> Other address: Xing Hua City, Jiang Su Province, China
> Tel: 86-1234567
> Date of birth: 10. 13. 2005
> Email:123456@qq.com
> Nationality: China

UNIT 7 Application Materials

> **EDUCATION AND QUALIFICATIONS**
>
> 2023–2025, Harbin Institute of Technology, BSc. (Hons.) in Electrical Engineering
>
> Subjects include: University Mathematics, Physics
>
> My project involved test automation techniques, which required independent research skills.
>
> 2020–2023, No.1 High School
>
> **WORK EXPERIENCE**
>
> 2023, Worked for the McDonalds' in XX City. Duties include…
>
> **CERTIFICATES/ SKILLS/ HONORS**
>
> - Programming skills in C Programming Language
> - Good level of some sports
> - Certificate in College English Test Band 4
> - Full clean driving license
>
> **ACTIVITIES AND INTERESTS**
>
> - Singing songs and playing basketball
> - I enjoy animation and am a member of HIT Animation Club
> - Other interests include listening to music and reading novels

Activity 3 Questions About PS/SOP Writing

The following questions should be asked when you are writing your PS or SOP. Some of them are about the content of your PS, some are about structure, and some are about style. Read the questions and group them into their categories.

1) Are you showing off rather than telling?
2) Does your introduction grab the reader's attention?
3) Do you explore your experience deeply enough?
4) Does your PS/SOP contain specific details and concrete evidence?
5) Does your PS/SOP reveal anything unique about your character?
6) Can you identify an overarching theme?
7) Do you have a reason for placing every paragraph where it is?
8) Do your paragraphs flow smoothly? Are there any gaps or jumps?
9) Does each point build upon previous points, or does your PS/SOP sound like a list?

10) Have you written insightful transitions and resolutions that highlight your key themes?
11) Have you kept a simple and straightforward style?
12) Have you varied your sentence constructions?
13) Have you avoided using unnecessary fancy vocabulary?
14) Have you avoided using passive voice?
15) Have you achieved active writing through the use of strong verbs?

Content:

Structure:

Style:

Activity 4 Careful Reading of Cover Letters

Read and compare the following two cover letters. Then discuss with your partner and decide which one is better and why.

Letter A:

> Respected Sir,
>
> I am looking forward to going to the US for further study. I am seeking admission and financial assistance from your esteemed university. I am very interested in artificial intelligence and computer architecture. I have programming experience in C++, C and Java. I am also familiar with several software packages in the Windows environment (MS Word, Excel Spreadsheet, etc.). My GRE score is high, and I got 99 in the TOEFL exam.
>
> I request you to spare a few minutes of your precious time to go through the resumé I have attached.
>
> Sir, if you are kind enough to offer me an assistantship, I promise to work very hard for you. I have a very good academic record since primary school. By the way, can you tell me what my chances are of getting an assistantship from your department?

UNIT 7 Application Materials

> Can you kindly inform me about the last date for Summer Term next year before which I can apply?
>
> Thank you for your valuable time.
>
> Yours obediently,
>
> Student A

Letter B:

> Dear Prof. Smith,
>
> I am applying to ASU (amongst other places) for a Ph.D, and I am very interested in your research areas. I would like to explore the possibility of doing my research with you, with financial support.
>
> One possible area that would interest me a lot is applying Tikhonov Regularization to your problem in computational neuroscience, since I understand that neural data can be very noisy, and yet sparse. Alternately, I am also interested in applying evolutionary algorithms to your genetic neural network parameter estimation. One of my other interests is in parallel processing. Are you considering parallel implementations for any of your optimization/ estimation algorithms? Considering that the projects that you list in your website would probably be very computationally intensive, that may be a worthwhile strategy to pursue.
>
> I presented a paper entitled "Hybrid Gradient Descent Based Training of Probabilistic Recurrent Networks" at the International Conference on Neural Networks and Image Processing held in Beijing last year. It is a reviewed publication. I have attached a copy of the article in PDF format.
>
> If you have available funds and are interested in my application, please let me know soon.
>
> Sincerely,
>
> Student B

Activity 5 Making a Short Presentation

Make a list of the materials you need to prepare before you send them to the admissions office of a famous university. Choose one of them and make a one-minute presentation in English about the important rules to remember when preparing it.

Section IV　Tool Box

1. **Useful Words and Expressions**

    1) Personal Information
        - 性别 gender
        - 出生地 place of birth
        - 生日 date of birth
        - 通讯地址 address
        - 电话 telephone
        - 电子信箱 email
        - 国籍 nationality
        - 婚姻状况 marital status
        - 职业目标 career objective

    2) Educational Background
        - 课程 curriculum / subject
        - 主修专业 major
        - 辅修专业 minor

    3) Experience
        - 发表论文 publication
        - 专利 patent
        - 科研项目 research project
        - 志愿服务 voluntary service
        - 兼职工作 part-time job
        - 实习 internship
        - 勤工俭学 work-study program
        - 义教 voluntary teaching

    4) Honorable Title
        - 三好学生 Three-Virtue Student / Merit Student

- 优秀毕业生 Outstanding Graduate
- 先进班集体 Advanced Class
- 学生会优秀干部 Outstanding Cadre of Student Union
- 学生会优秀个人 Outstanding Individual of Student Union
- 精神文明先进个人 Advanced Individual in Promoting Ethical Progress
- 优秀青年志愿者 Outstanding Young Volunteer
- 社会工作先进个人 Advanced Individual in Social Work
- 十大学生修身楷模 Top Ten Model Students of Self-Cultivation
- 校园十杰 Ten Prominent Youth on Campus / Top Ten Youth on Campus
- 十佳社团 Top Ten Outstanding Associations

5) Award and Prize
- 国家奖学金 National Scholarship
- 国家励志奖学金 National Encouragement Scholarship
- 一等奖学金 The First Class Scholarship
- 人民奖学金 The People's Scholarship
- 学生科研创新奖 Student Award for Research and Innovation

6) Competition
- 英语演讲比赛 English Speech Contest
- 辩论邀请赛 Debate Invitational Competition
- 课件设计大赛 Courseware Design Competition
- 论文比赛 Essay Contest
- 全国数学建模比赛 National Mathematical Modeling Contest
- 创业大赛 Venture Contest
- 毕业设计大赛 Graduation Design Competition
- 实验技能操作大赛 Experiment Skill and Operation Contest
- 省级大学生科技竞赛 Provincial Science and Technology Contest for College Students
- 书画大赛 Chinese Calligraphy and Painting Competition

7) Extra Curriculum Activity
- 社会实践 social practice
- 学术活动 academic activity
- 政法论坛 Political and Legal Forum

- 迎新晚会 Welcome Party for the Freshmen
- 文化节 Culture Festival
- 学生会 Student Union

8) Skill and Credential
- 全国计算机等级考试 National Computer Rank Examination (NCRE)
- 驾驶证 driver's license

9) Language Proficiency
- 大学英语四级 CET-4 (College English Test Band 4 Certificate)
- 英语专业八级 TEM-8 (Test for English Major Grade 8 Certificate)
- 普通话等级考试 National Mandarin Test (Level 1, 2, 3; Grade A, B, C)
- 雅思 IELTS (International English Language Testing System)
- 托福 TOEFL (Test of English as a Foreign Language)
- 剑桥商务英语证书考试 BEC (Business English Certificate)

2. Useful Information

1) There are countless samples on the Internet. Studying some good examples of application documents can be very helpful to you when you are preparing your own application materials, but you should always remember to write your own cover letter, CV and essay. In doing so, you not only produce a very original document in English, but also improve your writing skills.

2) The reference letters, or letters of recommendation, must be written by the referees. The referees must know you quite well and be willing to recommend you to support your application. You should first ask your advisors and professors to be your referees, and get their permission before you write down their names and contact information.

3) Scan all your supporting materials, including your certificates, transcripts, publications and photos. Name the scanned files in English. Keep them in alphabetical order in a folder. Name the folder in English, for example, "Zhang San's Supporting Materials". Update this folder by adding new materials constantly. Always be prepared to supply them to the university or the company you are applying for.

UNIT 7 Application Materials

Section V Do You Know?

💬 Supplementary Readings

Read the following three passages and find out more about application materials. The answers to the questions at the beginning of each passage can be found through reading.

Passage 1 Application Materials for Stanford School of Business

> **Questions:**
> ♦ What are the necessary materials for a Ph.D program application?
> ♦ What does this passage say about reference letters?
> ♦ If you have graduated from a non-US university, will you be eligible for admission to this Ph.D program?

The Ph.D program application closes on December 1.

In this section, you will find all the information you need to complete your online application.

A complete application includes:
- Statement of purpose
- Resumé or CV
- Three letters of reference
- GMAT or GRE score
- TOEFL score (if applicable)
- Uploaded official transcripts
- Submitted online application
- $125 application fee

We strongly recommend that you and your referees submit your application and reference letters well before the application deadline. Remember to review your online application, including uploaded materials (e.g., resumé and statement of purpose), before submitting it.

Please do not mail an official transcript or additional materials (e.g., publications, photographs, videos, or portfolios) as part of your application.

Eligibility

To be eligible for admission to the Ph.D program, applicants must meet one of the following conditions:

- Completion of a bachelor's degree from a US college or university accredited by a regional accrediting association; or
- Completion of an international degree that is equivalent to a US bachelor's degree from a college or university of recognized standing. Please see the minimum international education requirements.

We do not require the following as part of admissions:
- A minimum GPA (grade-point average)
- A minimum GMAT or GRE score
- Particular fields of undergraduate/graduate study
- A minimum level of work experience
- MBA or other graduate degrees

Passage 2 Comparison Between a CV and a Cover Letter

Questions:
- What is a CV?
- What is a cover letter?
- What are the differences between a CV and a cover letter?
- Is there any similarity between a CV and a cover letter?

A cover letter is brief while a CV is quite detailed and long. A CV includes detailed information about your work experience and academic background while a cover letter is a condensed document that explains why you're applying for the given job.

UNIT 7 Application Materials

But let's park that for a minute and break it down.

What Is a CV?

That actually depends on where you are.

In the US, a CV is a very detailed document that lists your work experience, skills, educational background along with other academic achievements and it is used by people pursuing a career in academia.

In most of the rest of the world, a CV is for a job and looks exactly like it's American resumé counterpart. It contains information on your work experience, skills, and educational background in reference to a particular job you're applying for.

For the sake of this article, we'll be using a CV to mean the curriculum vitae used in the academic community within the US.

A typical academic CV has the following content/information:

- Contact information
- Research profile
- Education section
- Publications
- Awards and honors
- Grants and fellowships
- Conferences
- Teaching experience
- Research experience
- Languages and skills

Impressive, no?

Given the large amount of information academic CVs contain, they can actually go on for several pages and it is considered standard in academia.

What Is a Cover Letter?

A cover letter is similar to what its name suggests—it's a letter that covers the key points in your experience and skill set that prove you're a great candidate for the job.

Unlike the bullet pointed list usually found on a CV, the cover letter reads like a letter and gives you an opportunity to deep dive into concrete examples of your expertise.

The general layout of a cover letter looks like this:

- Cover letter header
- Cover letter salutation
- Cover letter introduction
- Second paragraph that underlines your experience and expertise
- Third paragraph that proves you're a great fit to the company and role
- Cover letter ending with a call to action
- Professional sign-off

Compare this cover letter structure with the CV structure above and you can see how different they are.

CV vs. Cover Letter—The Differences

Generally, the focus of a CV is your value to academia, while a cover letter goes right for the feels.

But nothing clears things up like a nice table of values. Have a look at the table below to see a side-by-side comparison of the major differences between an academic CV and a cover letter.

	CV	Cover Letter
Presentation	Specific details	General information
Format	Lists and bullet points	Paragraphs and sentences
Length	May be several pages	Usually one page
Content	Facts and data	Examples and ideas
Purpose	Applying for academic jobs	Providing additional background information

But it's not only the differences between a CV and a cover letter that are important.

Let's see what makes them such a great pair.

CV vs. Cover Letter—The Similarities

Just like it takes two to tango on the ballroom floor, the CV usually takes the lead

UNIT 7 Application Materials

in the dance across the recruiter's desk. But without a cover letter, it's just one dancer swirling around with air.

Together they prove your skills and career experience—the CV lists them and the cover letter describes them in action through compelling examples.

The result is a holistic picture of your expertise and what kind of employee you are.

And think about it—the more the recruiter knows from the get-go, the more convinced he/she can be that you're the candidate he/she is looking for before you even step foot into the interview!

Plus, a great cover letter that matches your CV will give you an advantage over other candidates.

Let's do a quick recap of what we've covered in this passage:

- In the US, CVs are used in academia. In most of the rest of the world, a CV is used to get a job.
- Cover letters are letters that accompany CVs/resumés and go more in depth into your job experience and expertise.
- CVs are focused on facts and data about your work experience while cover letters are centered around compelling examples of your expertise as well as your character.
- A CV and cover letter deliver the most impact when they are tailored and sent together.

Passage 3 How to Write a Personal Statement

> **Questions:**
> ♦ What is essential for a successful personal statement?
> ♦ How long is a personal statement?
> ♦ What are the three aspects discussed in this passage about a personal statement?

What Is a Personal Statement?

A personal statement or autobiographical essay is a short essay that provides a relevant autobiographical account of your qualifications. The personal statement must serve as a reflection of your personality and intellect. You must sell yourself through this statement, just as you would through a successful job interview. Preparation and personal reflection are essential.

There is limit but it varies depending on the school and the program. Usually, personal statements are between 500-1,000 words long. Personal statement is an important part of the graduate school application. It provides the admission committee a chance to distinguish you from other A+ applicants and the opportunity to get to know you at a more personal level.

Your admissions essay can be the deciding factor in whether you are accepted or rejected by a school. Therefore, it is necessary that you write an essay that is honest, interesting, and well-structured.

The purpose of this guide is not to teach formulas, but rather to give the necessary direction for you to create an original and effective essay. We will teach you how to choose appropriate topics and themes, how to structure your essay as a coherent and flowing piece, and how to convey your ideas through engaging and active language.

Content

Here are some questions you can ask yourself when writing your personal statement.

- Have you been sincere and personal?
- Is your essay within the word limit?
- Will your reader find the essay interesting?
- Are you showing rather than telling?
- Does your introduction grab the reader's attention?
- Do you explore your experiences in sufficient depth?
- Does your essay contain a high level of detail and concrete evidence?
- Have you avoided unsubstantiated claims?

UNIT 7 Application Materials

- Do you offer specific, personal insights rather than trite generalizations and clichés?

- Does your essay reveal anything meaningful about your character?

- Do you avoid summarizing information that can be found elsewhere on your application?

- Will your essay make you stand out?

- Does your conclusion leave a lasting impression?

Structure

Some people can write well without thinking too much about structure. They naturally organize their information to be seamless, transitioning well between points and making their comments relevant to a theme. Most people, however, need to work at it a little more. Here are some very basic tips on how to make sure your personal statement has good structure.

Choose a Focus

It should be unique. It does not have to be life shattering, but you should be able to write about it with conviction, enthusiasm and authority.

It should be an experience you have some passion for. You must be able to support it as a "turning point" in your life. Ask yourself, "How did I change as a result of this experience?" For example, did it give you a new perspective or understanding; did it give you a new direction in life, or help you come to an important realization?

Don't limit yourself to thinking of experiences that can translate well into the moral of " ...and that's why I want to be a doctor". Choose something that you feel is truly representative of you, and something that you feel you can use to transition to other relevant aspects of your life. Otherwise, your statement may come off sounding staged or strained.

Create Strong Transitions

Transitions refer to the language you use to move from one idea to the next. Most of the time transitions are accompanied by a paragraph break. You should never assume, however, that a paragraph break is enough of an indication that you are

leaving one idea behind and moving on to another.

One way to check for clear transitions is to make sure the first sentence of every paragraph is somehow related to the last sentence in the previous paragraph. Even when you need to shift gears pretty drastically, you should find a way to create a "bridge" between your ideas.

If you have chosen a strong focus and frame, your transitions will be much easier. This is because you can use your frame and focus as a sort of hub that is the origin of each new idea that you choose to explore in your statement.

In addition to making sure that you transition well between your ideas, you should also make sure that your ideas are presented in a logical order that your reader can identify and follow. Many students choose to use a chronological order.

You might choose to order things from most to least important, or categorize your ideas (e.g., academics, volunteer experience, work experience, etc.). Whatever order you choose, be faithful to it.

It should be sustainable throughout your statement. In other words it has to have enough depth and flexibility to carry you through your statement while avoiding repetition. The details of the event should afford you opportunity to talk about related experiences that you want the people who are considering you for an interview to know.

Check the following list to see if your transition is well-written.

- Can you identify an overarching theme? Have you articulated that theme in the essay?

- Does your theme have multiple layers and genuine depth?

- Do you have a reason for placing every paragraph where it is?

- Do your paragraphs flow smoothly? Are there any gaps or jumps?

- Does each point build upon previous points, or does your essay sound like a list?

- Have you written insightful transitions and resolutions that highlight your key themes?

- Are your stories well integrated into your essay?

UNIT 7 Application Materials

- Is the essay clear and coherent? Have you strengthened its impact by using the optimal structure?

Style

Check the following list to see if you're using the right style.

- Have you achieved a simple, straightforward style?
- Have you varied your sentence constructions?
- Have you avoided unnecessarily fancy vocabulary?
- Have you avoided passive voice?
- Have you achieved active writing through the use of strong verbs?
- Have you avoided overusing adjectives and adverbs?
- Is your tone conversational, rather than too casual or too formal?
- Have you conveyed confidence, enthusiasm, and passion?

UNIT 8

Studying Abroad

Learning Objectives

After learning this unit, you will be able to:
- predict the difficulties you may encounter while studying abroad and prepare solutions;
- compare the cultural differences in terms of college life;
- build up confidence for a possible future college life abroad;
- comprehend the value of independence and self-discipline in the life of studying abroad.

Section I Warm-Up

1. If you can have your way, what university outside of China would you like to study at? Why do you choose this one? Tell your reasons to your partner.
2. Do you think it is a good thing for a person to study abroad? What benefits can that bring? Are there disadvantages? Discuss with your partner.
3. Write down as many as you can the possible problems you will have when studying abroad, and compare your notes with your partner's.

_____
_____
_____
_____

Section II Points to Remember

There are important points to remember and some rules to follow in present-day international communication. The following is a summary of the basics in regard to studying abroad. Referring to these points constantly may help you study abroad more successfully.

Part 1 Campus Life

1. **Advice on Your Arrival**
   - Find the international office (or the foreign affairs office), which is usually responsible for international admissions, designing programs for international students, organizing social activities, and providing all around assistance to international students.
   - Don't miss the freshmen orientation.
   - Do the registration.
   - Pay your fees and tuition.
   - Meet your student advisor (or your supervisor).

UNIT 8 Studying Abroad

- Get familiar with your surroundings.

2. How to Study Your Courses
- Complete courses for credits, graduation, certificate or diploma.
- In UK or US universities, choose 3 or 4 courses per semester, especially not too many in the first semester.
- Take a writing course, an introductory course, a foundational course to your major, and a challenging course leading you to a specialty.
- Your final grade for a course is usually calculated based on your attendance, participation, homework, projects, teamwork, quizzes and exams. Grading methods vary from course to course.
- Before classes, read all the articles and chapters on the reading list from your professor.
- Listen to lectures carefully, take notes, and write summaries or commentaries.
- Join class discussions and make presentations actively.
- Meet your professors in tutorials to ask questions and have discussions with them.
- Go to seminars. Listen and learn.
- Maintain academic integrity and never cheat on exams or homework.
- Understand what plagiarism is and avoid it in writing your essay.

3. Tips for Success in College
- Don't pay too much attention to how other people might see you. Learn with an open mind.
- Remember that making mistakes is a natural thing. That's an essential part of the learning experience.
- Make sure that you speak slowly and clearly so that everyone can hear you.
- Make sure that you speak up and everyone understands you.

Part 2 Personal Life

1. Achieving Independence
- Make decisions independently.
- Study independently.
- Look after yourself, and learn to do shopping, cook, clean, go to the hospital, etc.,

all by yourself.
- Get over loneliness.
- Make some new friends.

2. Cope with Culture Shock
   - Feelings of isolation, confusion and doubt are all parts of culture shock.
   - Meeting people and getting to know your host culture are important to make you feel more at home.
   - Keep in touch with family back home.
   - Alcohol and shopping are just temporary fixes to numb feelings of homesickness.
   - Getting to know more about your new culture, language, history, and environment will have a positive influence on you.

3. Preparations Before Leaving Home
   - Learn to think and do things independently.
   - Learn to cope with difficulties.
   - Find some effective ways to overcome loneliness and sadness, such as sports, food, movies and music.
   - Know whom to turn to for help in an emergency.
   - Learn about your future school, university, institution or program.
   - Learn about the people you are going to work with, study with or live with, and communicate with them beforehand.
   - Get information about campus life from school websites, or from blog articles.
   - Prepare yourself with some practical skills in life, such as cooking, driving, cleaning and firstaid.
   - Sharpen your computer and Internet skills.
   - Learn to manage time effectively.
   - Improve your language and communication skills.

Part 3   Social Life

1. How to Join Clubs
   - There's generally a strong effort in overseas universities to encourage students to join clubs and many students will join clubs.
   - Club life is an important part of international students' experience.

UNIT 8 Studying Abroad

- An important part of students' resumé and CV padding is that they have some sort of extracurricular activity experience if they want a good job, want to take on some significant roles, or want some leadership and organizational experience.
- These clubs are easiest to discover in the first week of university.
- Almost every club will have a publicity stand, normally in the square. There will be banners and registration forms, shows and demonstrations on the stage, or videos or other things at the desk.
- Clubs will ask people, such as new students, to join them.
- They will send you an email with some more information after you sign up.
- It's more up to you to become an active member.
- After one semester, you might consider joining in a more proactive way, becoming a member that adds value to the club, or becoming a leader, a treasurer, a secretary, or someone who organizes things.

2. **Starting Your Own Club**
   - In foreign universities, clubs are organized, set up, led and completely run by students, with very little or no faculty involvement.
   - If you wish to set up your own club, the first step in most universities is to find the Student Union, which is the center of all the clubs and activities.
   - They will provide you with all the forms and information you need to set up your own club.
   - If you have an unusual hobby or interest, or perhaps you want to introduce some Chinese culture to the university in a way that they haven't experienced before, you can go to the Student Union and receptionists there will tell you to fill out some forms, what you need to do, whom to talk to, and they will organize a room for you.

Part 4 Essentials for a Chinese

The following are some additional rules to remember when you are studying abroad:
- Study really hard and realize your full potential.
- Be aware of the differences between Chinese universities and foreign universities,

and observe the rules and regulations there.
- Actively participate in class activities such as discussions, seminars and group work.
- Actively make friends, not only with Chinese, but also with local people.
- Always believe in yourself when it's hard. Have hope and determination and carry on.

And you can add more...

Section III Let's Do It!

Activity 1 Listening for Tips to Avoid Plagiarism

You are going to hear a short lecture named "Five Tips to Avoid Plagiarism". Listen carefully and take notes about these 5 tips.

1) _____

2) _____

3) _____

4) _____

5) _____

Activity 2 A Discussion About Safety Precautions

When we study abroad, we need to protect our life and property. What are the things we need to know in order to live and study abroad safely? The following are some tips to help you. Discuss with your partner(s) about them and choose three things that are the most important.

- Contact number of your supervisor at the university
- Contact person at the Chinese Embassy

UNIT 8 Studying Abroad

- Contact information of the local police station
- What to do in case of a fire, earthquake or other natural disasters
- Your parents' or spouse's mobile phone number
- A weapon such as a gun or a knife
- Chinese kung fu
- How to avoid dangerous places and people

Activity 3 Talking About Preparations

Imagine that you are going to study abroad in three months. Tell your partner what must be done before you go, why and how. The following are some tips to help you.
- Life necessities: shelter, food, clothing, transport, medicine, etc.
- Preparations for study: language, books, computer, stationery, etc.
- Social life: friends, family, classmates, professors.

Activity 4 Making a Short Presentation About a University

Search on the Internet and browse the webpage of an overseas university you wish to study at. Take notes of the aspects you are interested in, such as the structure of the university, teachers, programs, student life, and especially information about international students. Then make a 5-minute presentation of what you have found.

Activity 5 Understanding Paraphrases

When you write a research paper, you must cite your predecessors' theories, data or ideas. Paraphrasing is a very important way of citation, which is to restate other people's data or ideas using your own words. You can change the sentence structure, word use, or word order, but keep the original meaning. Remember to mention the original source and author. You'll be suspected of cheating if four consecutive words in a line are exactly the same as the original text.

Here is an example.

The original text says:
- Paraphrasing: A restating of someone else's thoughts or ideas in your own

words (Pears & Shields, 2013).

Bad paraphrasing (only changing a few words) will be:

- Paraphrase means restating of someone else's thoughts or ideas in your own words.

Good paraphrasing (using your own words and sentences to say again someone else's idea and give acknowledgement) should be like:

- According to Pears and Shields (2013), paraphrase is a restatement of another person's ideas or thoughts using your own words.

Now study the following two pieces of paraphrases and decide which is better and tell your partner why you think so.

Original Text:
- Because the intracellular concentration of potassium ions is relatively high, potassium ions tend to diffuse out of the cell. This movement is driven by the concentration gradient for potassium ions.

Paraphrase A:
- Because the intracellular concentration of potassium ions is high, potassium ions tend to diffuse out of the cell. This movement is triggered by the concentration gradient for potassium ions.

Paraphrase B:
- A textbook of anatomy and physiology reports that the concentration of potassium ions inside of the cell is relatively high and, consequently, some potassium tends to escape out of the cell.

Section IV Tool Box

1. **Useful Words and Expressions**
   - 国际学生，留学生 international student/overseas student
   - 交换项目 exchange program
   - 学生辅导员 student advisor
   - 导师 supervisor
   - 面对面辅导 tutorial

UNIT 8 Studying Abroad

- 讨论会 seminar
- 讲座 lecture
- 阅读书目 reading list
- 记笔记 note-taking
- 论文 research paper/paper/essay
- (硕士)学位论文 thesis
- (博士)学位论文 dissertation
- 口头报告，口头展示 oral presentation
- 助教 teaching assistant
- 助研 research assistant
- 期中考试 mid-term exam
- 期末考试 final exam
- 学分 credit
- 成绩单 transcript
- 文献综述 literature review
- 实验室 laboratory
- 基金 fund
- 奖学金 scholarship
- 志愿者 volunteer
- 实习 internship
- 学生会 Student Union
- 课余打工 moonlighting
- 兼职工作 part-time job
- 毕业 graduation

2. **Useful Sentences**

1) Asking for Opinions
   - Can you give me your thoughts on...?
   - Do you (dis)approve of...?
   - Do you agree with the opinion that...?
   - Do you have any views on...?
   - Do you share the/my view that...?
   - I'd like (to hear) your views on...

- What are your feelings about...?
- What are your views on...?
- I'd be (very) interested to hear your views on...
- What are your (first) thoughts on...?
- What would be your reaction if I said...?
- What's your position on...?
- Would it be right to say...?
- Would you support the view that...?

2) Giving Opinions
- I have no doubt that... / I'm certain that...
- I strongly believe that...
- I've never really thought about this before, but...
- My personal opinion is that... / Personally, my opinion is that...
- To be honest... / In my honest opinion, ...
- As far as I know, ...
- I agree with the opinion of...
- I could be wrong, but...
- I'd definitely say that...
- I'd guess/imagine that...
- I'd say that...
- I'm absolutely certain that...
- I'm fairly confident that...
- I'm no expert (on this), but...
- I'm positive that...
- I'm pretty sure that...
- It seems to me that...
- It's a complicated/difficult issue, but...
- My (point of) view (on this) is...

3) Agreeing
- So, we are / that is agreed.
- That makes sense (to me).
- Absolutely! /Exactly! /Precisely!

- I couldn't agree with you more.
- I feel/think that way, too.
- I guess so.
- I think everyone would agree with that.
- Okay, I was probably wrong.
- That answers all my questions.
- That is logical.
- That's (exactly) the way I see it (, too).
- That's (exactly/just) what I was going to say.
- That's (exactly/just) what I think.
- You've changed my mind.

4) Disagreeing
- I understand what you are saying, but…
- That's a good point, but…
- You could be right, but…
- (But) don't you think that…?
- (But) what about…?
- I don't really agree.
- I read something about this and…
- I used to think that (way)…, but…
- I'd like to agree (with you), but…
- I agree up to a point, but…

Section V Do You Know?

Supplementary Readings

Read the following three passages and find out more about international student life. The answers to the questions at the beginning of each passage can be found through reading.

Passage 1 How to Succeed in College

> **Questions:**
> ♦ What can you do to know your ultimate goal?
> ♦ Where can you go if you need help with research for a paper?
> ♦ Why is using a calendar or planner a necessity?
> ♦ What is an advantage of coming to class early and sitting in the front?

Success in college requires hard work, determination and the ability to persevere. Academic achievement will help you prepare for your career and become more sure of yourself as you consider your life goals. Think about your strengths and weaknesses as a student. If you're ambitious, committed to seeking help and willing to invest time in your class work, you'll realize success in college.

Setting Goals and Seeking Help

A list of short- and long-term goals serves as a road map for achievement in college. Begin by looking at the big picture and define what it will take to realize your ultimate goal. For example, if you want a career that requires graduate education, determine the college grade-point average you will need to be admitted to graduate school. If you're struggling in a class, take advantage of campus resources such as tutoring labs or study centers. For example, the Academic Success Center of Pitt Community College provides labs to help students with math, anatomy, English and writing. If you need help with research for a paper, go to the library and learn how to use the college's online database or interlibrary loan system. Reaching an academic goal requires a commitment to seek help and the drive to succeed.

Managing Time Effectively

Consider going to college like having a full-time job. This may seem strange given 12 semester hours of classes is only 12 hours in the classroom. However, since college is more rigorous than high school, you should expect to study two hours each week for every credit hour you're taking, according to Pitt Community College's article "How to Succeed in College". This means that 12 hours equals 36 hours of study and class time. To be successful, you'll need to commit to a structured schedule that includes classes, study time, a part-time job and recreation. If you choose to work, adjust your course load to ensure you have time to study. For example, Pitt Community College suggests limiting your course load to 10 to 12 hours if you work 20 hours per week or three to six credit hours if you work a full-time job. Using a calendar or planner is a necessity. This tool will help you track assignments, projects, papers and other class requirements.

Excelling in the Classroom

It may seem like a given, but attending every class is key to your success. If you're one of the first to arrive in class and sit in the front row, you'll demonstrate an excitement to learn. Your professors will recognize you as an engaged student if you keep your cellphone in your backpack and only use your laptop when it's needed for the class. It's important to turn in your assignments on time and meet the details of the rubrics. Do all you can to stand out in the class. For example, be the first to volunteer to lead a group project and complete extra credit assignments, if offered by your professor. If you have questions, don't hesitate to ask. Seeking answers develops a connection with your professors.

Taking Care of Health

Personal wellness impacts your ability to concentrate and perform well in the classroom. Be proactive and develop healthy habits by scheduling personal time to exercise, sleep and eat three meals each day. Students who avoid a wellness routine are more likely to have trouble succeeding in college. For example, if you schedule social time late at night, knowing you have an 8 am class, you're less likely to be able to concentrate or even make it to class at all. Most colleges provide student services and resources to provide support for nonacademic needs. If you're feeling overwhelmed by the rigor of college classes, seek help from a mentor or college resource center. For example, Monash University encourages students who have personal concerns to take advantage of the counseling center.

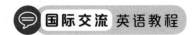

Passage 2 How to Avoid Plagiarism

> **Questions:**
> ♦ What is plagiarism?
> ♦ Why is it so difficult to avoid plagiarism?
> ♦ What is common knowledge?
> ♦ What will too many quotations lead to?

According to Merriam-Webster Dictionary, "plagiarize" means:

"To steal and pass off (the ideas or words of another) as one's own to use (another's production) without crediting the source;

To commit literary theft to present as new and original an idea or product derived from an existing source."

Plagiarism is one of the most severe violations of academic writing. It may have serious consequences for a student and even expulsion from college/university. In order not to expose yourself to such unjustified risk, remember rule No. 1 — avoid any form of plagiarism while writing an essay.

Sometimes it is especially difficult because of the specific nature of essay writing itself.

On the one hand, you should show that you have conducted a in-depth research, but on the other hand, you should demonstrate a brand new perspective of the suggested topic. You should refer to authoritative sources, but at the same time express your own opinion.

It does not matter to your professor whether you plagiarize incidentally or deliberately. To be on the safe side — remember rule No. 1.

First of all, avoiding plagiarism in essays implies citing sources. You do not have to do this only when the idea is a common fact for the intended audience.

Common knowledge is something that:

- your reader already knows;
- can easily be found in general reference sources;
- is not cited in other sources.

To avoid plagiarism, you should start documenting the sources as early as you start doing your research.

In your draft, mark the ideas that are yours and those which are drawn from other sources. Underline, italicize someone else's words in your notes. As you are paraphrasing, try not to peep into the primary source, and write from memory. Check and correct possible inaccuracies. Paraphrase should acknowledge the author, e.g., according to... If you want to keep a particular phrase, do not fail to use quotation marks with it.

Limit the general number of direct quotations to the most powerful ones. Your writing will lose its own voice and identity when stuffed with too many direct quotes.

Passage 3 Citing Sources

Questions:
- What are the benefits of citing your source?
- How many formats of citation are discussed in the passage?
- How do you know which format of citation to use when doing research?

When using another author's intellectual property (from primary or secondary source material), it is essential that you properly cite your sources. Giving credit not only benefits your credibility as an author, but will also help you avoid plagiarism. Be sure to carefully document all the necessary citation information for your sources while doing your research to make the process much easier.

There are multiple formats of citation styles, and they vary according to academic discipline. The Modern Language Association (MLA) has a specific format for citation information that is to be included both in the text and on a Works Cited page. This format is used in English and some other humanities courses, including stylistic conventions for essay formatting as well as citations.

Similarly, the American Psychological Association (APA) has its own form of citation and formatting that is most often utilized in social science courses. Yet another style of citation is the Chicago Manual of Style, which is often used in research papers in history and some humanities courses.

You should always check with your professor about which citation format to use.

UNIT 9

International Conference

Learning Objectives

After learning this unit, you will be able to:

- understand meeting etiquette;
- analyze situations of international conferences and know how to prepare for an international conference;
- create an introduction to how to organize an international conference;
- write a meeting agenda and meeting minutes.

Section I Warm-Up

1. When you write an invitation, what kind of information should be included?

2. What should you do when you receive guests before a meeting?

Section II Points to Remember

There are important points to remember and some rules to follow when organizing an international conference. The following is a summary of the basics in regard to meeting etiquette, preparing for a conference, organizing a conference, receiving participants and writing a meeting agenda and meeting minutes. Referring to these points constantly may help you behave well in an international conference.

Part 1 Meeting Etiquette

- Be polite when interrupting and disagreeing with others.
- Show respect in a professional and non-confrontational way.
- Use words like "can", "could", "would like", "sorry", "just", "I think", "I feel", etc.
- Acknowledge people by using their names, or words like "you", "we", "everybody", "my colleagues", etc.
- Prepare well for the meeting by studying the agenda, researching the topics to be discussed, and preparing the vocabulary to be used.
- Familiarize yourself with the terms and expressions to be used at the meeting.

UNIT 9 International Conference

💬 Part 2 Preparing for a Conference

1. **Specifying the Features of the Conference**
   - What kind of a conference is it?
   - For whom is the conference organized?
   - Who should and should not be invited?
   - Where will it be held?
   - When will it be held?
   - How long will it be?

2. **Drafting Invitations for Applicants**
   - Type of conference.
   - Date.
   - Time.
   - Length.
   - Venue.
   - Theme and topics.
   - Participants.
   - Organizers.
   - Applications deadline.
   - Cost.

💬 Part 3 Organizing a Conference

1. **Management of the Organizational Team (the Most Demanding Task)**
   - Divide tasks among members properly.
   - Monitor progress and how things are developing.

2. **Finance**
   - Find some sponsorship.
   - Make a budget.
   - Look for other means of support.

3. **Meeting Program**
   - Plan what to do during the event.
   - Contact possible speakers.
   - Prepare a contingency plan.

4. Accommodation
   - Comfortable and convenient.
   - Near the meeting venue.
   - At reasonable prices.

5. Checking Progress of Organizational Tasks
   - Conduct regular meetings.
   - Set up deadlines for different tasks.
   - Contact with participants.

Part 4 Receiving the Participants

- Prepare for the arrival of the participants.
- Meet with the heads of delegations.
- Arrange a warm reception.
- Hold daily planning meetings.

Part 5 Writing a Meeting Agenda and Meeting Minutes

1. Meeting Agenda
   - List of meeting participants.
   - Minutes of the last meeting.
   - Matters arising from the minutes of the last meeting.
   - Agenda subjects.
   - Other matters.
   - Date, time, place of the next meeting.
   - Adjournment.

2. Meeting Minutes
   - An accurate and concise record of what happened.
   - Information recorded in the third person and past tense.
   - The names of the chairperson, secretary and all other attendants.
   - The signature of chairperson.
   - Date.

UNIT 9 International Conference

Part 6 Essentials for a Chinese

The following are some rules to remember when you organize an international conference:

- Practice meeting etiquette.
- Prepare well for the conference.
- Arrange a warm reception for your guests.
- Provide nice and cozy accommodation for guests.
- Keep in touch with your participants all the time.
- Provide an accurate and concise record of what happened.

And you can add more...

Section III Let's Do It!

Activity 1 Organizing an International Conference

Prepare a three-minute speech entitled "How to Organize an International Conference". Present your speech in a small group of 4–5 people. The best in the group should go to the front and make the speech to the class. You can write down keywords or an outline of your speech in the space below.

How to Organize an International Conference

Beginning:

___

Body:

___

Ending:

Activity 2 Designing a Conference Poster

Read the passage "Call for Papers" on Pages 184–187 and discuss with your group how to design a conference poster. Then give a draft of the poster in the space below.

Activity 3 Giving a Presentation

Make a group discussion to sum up some Dos and Don'ts of giving a presentation and fill in the blanks.

Dos	Don'ts

UNIT 9 International Conference

Activity 4 Writing a Meeting Agenda

Suppose the company you work for will have a meeting and participants are the heads of different departments. Write a meeting agenda.

Meeting Agenda

_____
_____
_____
_____
_____
_____
_____
_____
_____
_____

Activity 5 Translating Meeting Minutes

Suppose you are the secretary of a company. Write down the monthly meeting minutes in English with the following information.

1. 开会时间：20XX 年 8 月 20 日下午四点
2. 开会地点：会议室
3. 主持人：Mr. Black
4. 出席者：Mr. Stone, Mr. White, Ms. Green, Ms. Sun, Mr. Lee
   缺席者：Mr. Jordon
5. 会议内容：讨论 12 月 30 日在 Newtown Restaurant 举办新年聚会的安排；选举董事会顾问成员；讨论新员工培训方案，由人事经理 Ms. Green 主持
6. 下次会议时间：20XX 年 10 月 19 日（时间地点相同）
7. 会议结束时间：下午五点

_____
_____
_____
_____

Section IV Tool Box

1. **Useful Words and Expressions**

   1) Meeting
      - 论坛，讨论会 forum
      - 专题讨论会，研讨会 symposium
      - 研讨会，讲习班 workshop
      - （大型正式）会议 conference
      - 年会 annual convention
      - 研讨会，培训会 seminar
      - 座谈小组 panel
      - 辩论会 debate
      - 网络会议 webinar

   2) International Conference
      - 征稿 call for abstract/proposal/paper
      - 会议举办地点 conference location/venue
      - 会议日程安排 conference schedule/program
      - 注册截止日期 deadline/closing date for registration
      - 提交截止日期 submission deadline
      - 欢迎宴会 welcome banquet
      - 开幕式 opening ceremony/session
      - 全体大会 plenary session
      - 主旨会议 keynote session

UNIT 9 International Conference

- 主旨演讲 keynote speech
- 口头展示 oral presentation
- 分组会议 parallel session
- 海报展示 poster presentation
- 问答环节 question and answer session
- 茶歇 tea/coffee break
- 闭幕式 closing ceremony

2. Useful Sentences

1) Giving a Presentation

- It's a pleasure for me to make this presentation here to you.
- In today's presentation I'd like to show you...
- The purpose of my presentation is to inform you of...
- My presentation is going to cover three points...
- I've divided my talk into four main parts/sections...
- Firstly, ... After that we will look at... And finally I'll...
- First, I am going to tell you something about the background... / give you some facts and figures...
- After that, we'll look at the advantages and disadvantages of...
- Then, I'll move on to...
- Well, let's move on to the second point.
- That brings me to my third point.
- I'd then like to conclude with...
- In this concluding section, I want to discuss briefly...
- Finally, I'd like to finish by thanking you for your attention.
- Thank you for your attention / for inviting me here today.

2) Asking Questions

- I would like to ask/address/raise a question about...
- I wonder if you would like to explain/comment on the point of...
- Do you mind showing me whether/why/how/what/when...?
- I could not understand what you really mean by...
- Could you provide any example to prove what you have said about...?

3) Answering Questions
- I am not quite sure what your question is. Could you address your question more specifically?
- I don't know whether I have understood your question correctly. Do you mean...?
- That is just what I mean.
- That is not what I mean.
- Sure/Absolutely/Certainly/Definitely.
- No, absolutely/certainly/definitely not.
- I'm in complete agreement / I (quite) agree / I couldn't agree more.
- I'd like to present/offer/give/express/state my opinion on...
- In my opinion, the conclusion can be supported by the experimental result that...
- As far as I know, little in-depth research has been carried out yet. I can only provide a partial answer to that question.
- I think the answer to the question needs some further study. I'm afraid it's not within the field of the presentation.
- I'm sorry my experience/knowledge about your question is very limited so I think I cannot give a good answer to your question.
- I can't fully remember. I'll have to check up on it.

4) Inviting Comments
- I wonder whether my question is helpful to you.
- Is my explanation clear enough?
- Is that what you wanted me to answer?
- Would anyone like to add anything (to what I've said)?
- Would anyone care to comment?
- Would anyone like to give their ideas on this?
- Would anyone care to add their thoughts (to the discussion)?

UNIT 9 International Conference

Section V Do You Know?

Supplementary Readings

Read the following three passages and find out more about international conferences. The answers to the questions at the beginning of each passage can be found through reading.

Passage 1 How to Organize a Conference

Questions:
- When should you begin planning the conference?
- Who is a conference coordinator?
- When are conferences usually held in Europe?
- What should you consider when choosing your conference venue?
- What should be included on the conference website?
- How can you encourage early registration?

A conference is a great way for people with a common interest to get together and exchange the most cutting-edge ideas in their field. Conferences are regular occurrences in academia, many industry fields, and multi-level marketing groups, to name a few. If you have decided to organize a conference in your area, you might be starting to realize that a well-planned conference has a to-do list about a mile long. There is the conference venue, participant list, materials, technology and even refreshments to think about and plan. If you are beginning to regret stepping up to plan, slow down, take a breath and know that you have the skills to organize a conference. The key to successful conference planning is to take each task one step at a time, and keep a thorough list of what you've done and what you need to do next.

Planning the Conference: Early Stages

1) Start early. You should begin early stages of planning the conference at least

eight months in advance, even longer if the conference will have many participants or is large in scope.

Remember, many venues and catering services must be reserved months in advance, and many participants will have to travel and make scheduling arrangements to be present.

Furthermore, you might need sponsors and large companies prepare their annual budgets months in advance so any financial or non-financial help has to be negotiated with them in advance.

2) Form a committee. A conference committee makes all the decisions for the conference, and having more than one person ensures that you have enough perspectives to make decisions on important issues and that you have enough people to actually pull off the details.

You will need a conference coordinator, who is the point person for all the major decisions and who will end up giving the most time to pulling everything together. You can also hire an event planner if you have a big enough budget, and spare yourself the headache.

If this conference is to repeat one that has been held before, try to get the previous year's coordinator on the committee. If he or she cannot participate, at least ask for any materials from the previous year to help planning.

3) Write down your goals and agenda. You will need to clearly define what you hope to accomplish with this conference because this will shape the rest of your decisions. Knowing what you want to convey and to whom before you begin any other conference organizing eases the stress of moving forward.

If you have never planned a conference, it is wise to stick to a small and relatively straightforward plan the first time you attempt it. Practically speaking, that means a conference of one or two days at the most, with no more than 250 to 300 people.

4) Choose the city and the dates. Although you may not be able to choose the specific date and location without more planning, it's important that you have a good idea of how much time you have to plan.

There are likely a lot of constraints on the date that you choose owing to your particular situation, but in general, conferences are usually held during particular times of the year and particular days of the week. In Europe, for example, conferences are usually held between March and June or between September and November. Similarly, conferences tend to be held from Thursday to Friday or Monday to Tuesday. Find out what the industry norms are in your area before choosing the month and days.

The length of a conference depends on how many people you think will be participating, and what all needs to be accomplished at a conference. For a conference of 250 to 300 people, plan for about two full days.

In general, you should only attempt to organize a conference in your own city, and the city needs to have access to a nearby airport, hotels, and an acceptable choice of venues. It's best, too, if the city is a large metropolitan area that people would want to visit anyhow; people on the fence about attending a conference are more likely to go if it is in a tourist destination.

5) Name the conference. This will help when you begin publicizing, but also helps in planning since you can keep your materials consistent and start building a social media presence for the conference.

Choose a name that hints at the goal and/or audience of the conference itself. Look up names of similar conferences to get ideas, but be sure yours is original and not sounding similar to another event.

Organizing the Conference

1) Develop your budget. There is no way that you can do anything else without knowing how much money you have to spend overall, and then breaking that down into allocations such as conference venue, materials and speakers' fees. Stick to your budget, and if you delegate responsibilities, make sure your assistants are adhering to their monetary limits as well.

The budget might be influenced by whether or not you want to try to recruit sponsors for your event. Sponsors pay a fee to support the conference, but also get a say in the content of the conference itself, typically including hosting presentations or panels with their own speakers and branding conference materials with their logos. On the plus side, a sponsor pays you up front, which gives you more money to work with as you plan. Sponsors might include local industry leaders or philanthropists, depending on your topic.

2) Establish ticket price and method of sales. Some conferences are free to participants, and others charge fees. There are several factors to consider when setting the ticket price and determining how to begin selling tickets:

What are the fees associated with conference planning? If it is a small, local conference with little or no fees, it might make sense not to charge people for attending. Another option is to allow people who present to attend free, while others pay a small fee to cover conference costs.

Multi-day conferences or those that serve meals typically charge registration fees, which can vary from $30 to several hundred in the United States.

Many conferences use a sliding pay scale for people in different stages of their careers. For example, academic conferences typically charge a lower fee for students than for faculty, and also charge a lower fee for members of the sponsoring association than for the general public.

3) Choose your conference venue. When looking for locations, keep in mind the number of participants, the convenience of the location, parking and proximity to public transportation, airports and hotels. Your goal in finding a place to hold the conference should be making it as easy as possible for participants to attend.

Check out whether your city has a convention center or hotel with convention rooms. For small conferences, you can often rent a community center.

4) Enlist the help of venue staff. If you have chosen a venue that is known for holding conferences, then tap into this invaluable resource. This is what the staff does every day and should be able to answer any questions or concern and provide advice when needed.

Some venues even have an event planner on staff who can handle many of the remaining details of your conference. Even if the planner charges a fee, it may be worth it to prevent this from becoming your own full-time job for the next few weeks.

5) Decide on a menu. When you organize a conference, you need to remember that participants will not want to sit all day without eating a decent meal, and many

won't know what is available in the area. Figure out if you will be hiring a catering service to bring in breakfast, lunch and snacks or if the conference venue you have chosen will provide food service.

Keep in mind that many people have dietary restrictions and preferences that can make planning meals rather difficult. If you choose an experienced caterer, it can create options for vegetarian, nut-free, gluten-free, or other meal preferences.

6) Insist on a walk-through. After you have gotten through the bulk of your conference organizing, don't leave anything to chance by walking in with the rest of the participants when the conference is set to begin.

Go to the conference venue and meet with the staff the day before to be certain that everything is in place and to take care of any last-minute details.

Planning the Contents of the Conference

1) Plan the schedule. You already know the title of the conference and have a general idea of the topics. But now you have to decide how it will actually play out. Conferences come in many types, and different industries take different approaches. If you are unsure how to proceed, consider going with a common conference format.

Begin with a keynote or opening address. This is usually a speech or presentation given by a huge name in the industry or field—whoever happens to be the most well-known speaker you can convince to come. The keynote can take place in the evening, and then end with a dinner, or it can take place first thing in the morning on the first day of the conference.

The remaining day or days of the conference should be divided into shorter sessions. The actual content of sessions is usually determined by who is planning to attend (participants will submit proposals), but you can also plan for workshops, film screenings, or other formats that you know you want to include. Depending on how many people are attending, you can have one session happening at one time (which is called "plenary") or you can have several sessions running concurrently (called "breakout groups") so that participants have a choice of what to attend.

End the conference on a high note, with a motivational speaker or a challenge to the audience.

2) Decide what type of sessions to have. These will vary depending on industry standards, but you might consider lectures, works-in-progress presentations, workshops, policy updates or state-of-the-field addresses, interactive sessions, or open-floor poster presentations.

The type of sessions you expect to have will influence how you publicize the conference, so decide early what type of content will be most meaningful to your target audience.

Sessions can range from 45 minutes to three hours each, depending on the number of presentations and the content.

3) Plan if you need to include any other activities. Figuring out how to fit other important events into your conference schedule is vital for a successful event.

You can also schedule time for organizational business such as business meetings or awards.

You can include catered meals or ask attendees to bring a brown-bag meal (generally, only choose the last option if you are not charging a fee for attendance; otherwise, people will expect their registration fees to cover at least one meal). You can also take a break and let attendees get lunch at nearby establishments, if your venue is in town.

Decide if your attendees are likely to want any type of entertainment, such as tours of the local area, a night at a comedy club, or a film or theater performance. In some cities and some industries, these are expected, but in others they might seem out of place.

Publicizing the Conference

1) Determine who will participate. There are many kinds of conferences, including academic, religious, and industry, and each of these types differs in types of participants. You need to be sure there is enough interest in the segment you are targeting before proceeding with planning.

If you are only targeting a small group, such as employees of your company or members of your church, you do not have to take as many steps to publicize the conference. A simple email or two, along with a mention in the newsletter and/or at administrative meetings should be enough to publicize the conference.

2) Find industry leaders to participate. You need a big headliner or keynote speaker to help convince other people in the industry.

Once you have confirmation that big names in the field will participate, you can include this information in your conference materials, such as your calls for participants.

3) Create a conference website. These days it is almost mandatory to have a digital presence for a successful conference. Find an available URL that includes the conference name or a logical derivative of it, so that it will be easy to find. Include all the important information about the conference at the website, and be sure to list the URL on all print materials and advertisements related to the conference.

On the website, be sure to include the date, time, and address of the conference venue, and names of any prominent speakers. You can also include information about transportation, lodging, area attractions, and you can attach the conference schedule when it is available, if desired.

You can also update the website with a link to register when you are ready to open up registration.

4) Advertise. Start early (up to a year in advance) so that presenters can begin submitting proposals for session ideas. Depending on the size of your conference and your target audience, your approach will differ. Keep in mind where members of your target audience get their information about this industry or group. These might include: social media, such as the sponsoring organization's Facebook page and Twitter feed; list-serves and e-mail contact lists; trade blogs, magazines, newsletters, or journals; posters, flyers, or other announcements sent to relevant groups, organizations, or businesses.

5) Solicit proposals. In your advertising materials, you should also include a "Call for Participants" or a "Call for Proposals" asking for individuals or groups to submit paper, panel, or workshop proposals.

Depending on your industry, you can ask for a specific length of the proposal. In academia, smaller conferences usually ask for an abstract of a few hundred words; larger conferences ask for entire manuscripts.

6) Begin accepting registrations. It's a good idea to have a way for participants to register before the conference, even months in advance, to give you an idea of how many people will show up.

Set up a registration website that is linked to the conference website. There are several ways to do this using existing services if you do not have the technical skills to create your own. For example, you can pay a fee to use the services of RegOnline, a company that hosts online registrations for events, compiles them, and sends them to you in a user-friendly way.

You can also allow participants to call or fax in their registrations if you have a way to process payment by credit card.

If you do not want to do an online or telephone method, create a registration form and upload it to your website as a PDF, then have participants print it and fill it out and mail it, along with a check, to your business address.

To encourage early registration, offer a discounted rate for those who register a month or more in advance, a slightly higher fee for waiting to register in the month prior to the conference, and a slightly higher fee for at-the-door registrations.

Passage 2 Call for Papers

Questions:
- When and where is the conference?
- What is ICICS short for?
- What does the conference aim at?
- How long should papers be?

ICICS 20XX

Chongqing, China, September 17–19, 20XX

Submission Deadline: May 11, 20XX

Dear Colleagues,

We cordially invite you to share your latest research results by submitting your manuscript to the ICICS 20XX that will be held in Chongqing, China on September 17–19, 20XX. Sorry for possible cross-posting.

———————————

CALL FOR PAPERS

ICICS 20XX (the International Conference on Information and Communications Security) will be held in Chongqing, China, on September 17–19, 20XX. It will be organized by Chongqing University, Xi'an Jiaotong University, and Peking University.

The conference started in 1997 and aims at bringing together leading researchers and practitioners from both academia and industry to discuss and exchange their experiences, lessons learned, and insights related to computer and communications security. More information about the previous conferences can be found at the official website.

Original papers offering novel research contributions on all aspects of information and communications security are solicited for submission to ICICS 20XX. There will be a Best Paper Award and a Best Student Paper Award. Areas of interest include, but are not limited to:

- Access control and authorization
- Anonymity
- Applied cryptography
- Attacks and defenses
- Authentication
- Biometrics security
- Block chains and distributed ledger security
- Censorship resistance
- Cloud security
- Cyber physical systems security
- Distributed systems security
- Economics of security and privacy
- Embedded systems security
- Forensics
- Hardware security

- Intrusion, detection and prevention
- Malware and unwanted software
- Mobile and Web security and privacy
- Language-based security
- Machine learning and AI security
- Network and systems security
- Privacy-preserving data mining
- Privacy technologies and mechanisms
- Protocol security
- Secure information flow
- Security and privacy for the Internet of Things
- Security and privacy metrics and policies
- Security architectures
- Social networks security, privacy and trust
- Software and application security
- Usable security and privacy
- Trustworthy computing

IMPORTANT DATES

Paper submission deadline: May 11, 20XX
Notification of acceptance: June 29, 20XX
Camera-ready due: July 13, 20XX
Conference: September 17–19, 20XX

INSTRUCTIONS FOR AUTHORS

Authors are invited to submit original papers not previously published nor submitted in parallel for publication to any other conference, workshop or journal. All submitted papers must be anonymous, with no author names, affiliations, acknowledgements, or obvious references.

Submissions should be in English, as a PDF file with all fonts embedded, in the Springer-Verlag LNCS format, typeset with 11pt font, and using reasonable spacing and margins.

Papers should not exceed 16 pages in LNCS style including the bibliography, but excluding well-marked appendices (no more than 18 pages in total). Note that papers should be intelligible without all appendices, since committee members are not required to read them. Submitted papers may risk being rejected directly without consideration of their merits if they do not follow all the above submission instructions.

Accepted papers will be presented at ICICS 20XX and included in the conference's post-proceedings which will be published by Springer in its Lecture Notes in Computer Science series. Please note that at least one author of each accepted paper should register with full rate to the conference and give a presentation at the conference. Failure to register or absence from the presentation will eventually make your paper not being included in the conference proceedings.

Passage 3 How to Write an Effective Title and Abstract and Choose Appropriate Keywords

> **Questions:**
> ♦ Why do the title, abstract and keywords play an important role in the communication of research?
> ♦ What are good research paper titles?
> ♦ What are different types of abstracts?
> ♦ What information is not included in an abstract?
> ♦ Why do you type your keywords into a search engine?

More often than not, when researchers set about writing a paper, they spend the most time on the "meat" of the article (the Methods, Results, and Discussion sections). Little thought goes into the title and abstract, while keywords get even lesser attention, often being typed out on-the-spot in a journal's submission system.

Ironically, these three elements—the title, abstract, and keywords—may well hold the key to publication success. A negligent or sloppy attitude towards these three vital elements in the research paper format would be almost equivalent to leaving the

accessibility of the research paper up to chance and lucky guessing of target words, indirectly making the effort and time expended on the research and publication process almost null and void.

It could be said that the keywords, title, and abstract operate in a system like a chain reaction. Once the keywords have helped people find the research paper and an effective title has successfully drawn in the readers' attention, it is up to the abstract of the research paper to further trigger the readers' interest and maintain their curiosity. This functional advantage alone serves to make an abstract an indispensable component within the research paper format.

However, formulating the abstract of a research paper can be a tedious task, given that abstracts need to be fairly comprehensive, without giving too much away. This is mainly because if readers get all the details of the research paper in the abstract itself, they might be discouraged from reading the entire article.

The Title, Abstract, and Keywords: Why It Is Important to Get Them Right

The title, abstract, and keywords play a pivotal role in the communication of research. Without them, most papers may never be read or even found by interested readers. Here's why:

- Most electronic search engines, databases, or journal websites will use the words found in your title and abstract, and your list of keywords to decide whether and when to display your paper to interested readers. Thus, these three elements enable the dissemination of your research; without them, readers would not be able to find or cite your paper.
- The title and abstract are often the only parts of a paper that are freely available online. Hence, once readers find your paper, they will read through the title and abstract to determine whether or not to purchase a full copy of your paper/ continue reading.
- Finally, the abstract is the first section of your paper that journal editors and reviewers read. While busy journal editors may use the abstract to decide whether to send a paper for peer review or reject it outright, reviewers will form their first impression about your paper on reading it.

Given the critical role that these three elements play in helping readers access your research, we offer a set of guidelines (compiled from instructions and resources on journals' websites and academic writing guidelines, listed in the references) on writing effective titles and abstracts and choosing the right keywords.

How to Write a Good Title for a Research Paper

Journal websites and search engines use the words in research paper titles to categorize and display articles to interested readers, while readers use the title as the first step to determining whether or not to read an article. This is why it is important to know how to write a good title for a research paper. Good research paper titles (typically 10–12 words long) use descriptive terms and phrases that accurately highlight the core content of the paper (e.g., the species studied, the literary work evaluated, or the technology discussed).

Here are some steps (with examples) you can follow to write an effective title:

1) Answer the questions: What is my paper about? What techniques/designs were used? What is studied? What were the results?

- My paper studies whether X therapy improves the cognitive function of patients suffering from dementia.
- It was a randomized trial.
- I studied 40 cases from six cities in Japan.
- There was an improvement in the cognitive function of patients.

2) Use your answers to list key words.
- X therapy
- Randomized trial
- Dementia
- 6 Japanese cities
- 40 cases
- Improved cognitive function

3) Build a sentence with these key words: This study is a randomized trial that investigates whether X therapy improved cognitive function in 40 dementia patients from 6 cities in Japan; it reports improved cognitive function (28 words).

4) Delete all unnecessary words (e.g., study of, investigates) and repetitive words;

link the remaining: This study is a randomized trial that investigates whether X therapy improved cognitive function in 40 dementia patients from 6 cities in Japan; it reports improved cognitive function randomized trial of X therapy for improving cognitive function in 40 dementia patients from 6 cities in Japan.

5) Delete non-essential information and reword: Randomized trial of X therapy for improving cognitive function in 40 dementia patients from 6 cities in Japan reports improved cognitive function.

Randomized trial of X therapy for improving cognitive function in 40 dementia patients (13 words): or (reworded with subtitle and a focus on the results); X therapy improves cognitive function in 40 dementia patients: A randomized trial (12 words).

How to Write a Research Paper Abstract

The abstract should work like a marketing tool. It should help the reader decide "whether there is something in the body of the paper worth reading" by providing a quick and accurate summary of the entire paper, explaining why the research was conducted, what the aims were, how these were met, and what the main findings were.

Types of Abstracts

Generally, between 100 and 300 words in length, abstracts are of different types: descriptive, informative, and structured.

Descriptive abstracts, usually used in the social sciences and humanities, do not give specific information about methods and results.

Informative abstracts are commonly used in the sciences and present information on the background, aim, methods, results, and conclusions.

Structured abstracts are essentially informative abstracts divided into a series of headings (e.g., Objective, Methods, Results, and Conclusion) and are typically found in medical literature and clinical trial reports.

In this section, we focus on how to write a research paper abstract that is concise and informative, as such abstracts are more commonly used in scientific literature. You can follow the same strategy to write a structured abstract; just introduce headings based on the journal guidelines.

UNIT 9 International Conference

How to Write An Abstract: Some Useful Tips

Begin writing the abstract after you have finished writing your paper.

First answer the questions "What problem are you trying to solve?" and "What motivated you to do so?" by picking out the major objectives and conclusions from your Introduction and Conclusion sections.

Next, answer the question "How did you go about achieving your objective?" by selecting key sentences and phrases from your Methods section.

Now, reveal your findings by listing the major results from your Results section.

Finally, answer the question "What are the implications of your findings?"

Arrange the sentences and phrases selected in steps and into a single paragraph in the following sequence: Introduction, Methods, Results, and Conclusion.

Make sure that this paragraph is self-contained, and does not include the following:

- Information not present in the paper
- Figures and tables
- Abbreviations
- Literature review or reference citations

Now, link your sentences.

Ensure that the paragraph is written in the past tense and check that the information flows well, preferably in the following order: purpose, basic study design/techniques used, major findings, conclusions, and implications.

Check that the final abstract:

- contains information that is consistent with that presented in the paper;
- meets the guidelines of the targeted journal (word limit, type of abstract, etc.);
- does not contain typographical errors as these may lead referees and editors to "conclude that the paper is bad and should be rejected".

How to Choose Appropriate Keywords in a Research Paper

Journals, search engines, and indexing and abstracting services classify papers using keywords. Thus, an accurate list of keywords will ensure correct indexing and help showcase your research to interested groups. This in turn will increase the chances of your paper being cited.

Here's how you can go about choosing the right keywords for your paper:

- Read through your paper and list down the terms/phrases that are used repeatedly in the text.
- Ensure that this list includes all your main key terms/phrases and a few additional key phrases.
- Include variants of a term/phrase (e.g., kidney and renal), drug names, procedures, etc.
- Include common abbreviations of terms (e.g., HIV).
- Now, refer to a common vocabulary/term list or indexing standard in your discipline and ensure that the terms you have used match those used in these resources.

Finally, before you submit your article, type your keywords into a search engine and check if the results that show up match the subject of your paper. This will help you determine whether the keywords in your research paper are appropriate for the topic of your article.

Conclusion

While it may be challenging to write effective titles and abstracts and to choose appropriate keywords, there is no denying the fact that it is definitely worth putting in extra time to get these right. After all, these three smallest segments of your paper have the potential to significantly impact your chances of getting published, read, and cited.

UNIT 10

Public Speaking

Learning Objectives

After learning this unit, you will be able to:
- understand the protocol of public speaking;
- learn about international communication skills regarding presentations, discussions, questions and answers;
- learn about how to deal with challenging situations in public speaking;
- learn about commonly used words and expressions for public speaking;
- learn about the rules of being non-offensive.

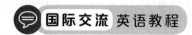

Section I Warm-Up

1. When delivering a presentation or listening to one, have you noticed the following common mistakes? Try to figure out the right way to put it.
    1) "I would like to start with a story / a funny joke."
    2) "Sorry / Excuse me if I seem nervous / I'm not good at public speaking."
    3) "Talk about" is used repeatedly or monotonously. (e.g., "First, I'll talk about competition. Then, I'll talk about Darwin. Then, I'll talk about Finches.")
    4) "Bear with me."
    5) "Sorry, let me rephrase."
    6) "The next slide shows / moves right along…"
    7) "I know this slide is really busy."
    8) "I think I've bored you enough / I didn't have enough time / That's all I have."
    9) "Um / uh / you know."
2. What are the common factors you need to consider before you begin preparing a public speech?
3. How can you make your presentation impressive?
4. List some of the important elements for an oral presentation.

Section II Points to Remember

There are important points to remember and some rules to follow in present-day international communication. The following is a summary of the basics in regard to presentations, discussions, questions and answers. Referring to these points constantly may help you to deliver an informative or persuasive speech.

Part 1 Presentation

1. Occasions
    - Academic conferences.
    - Business meetings.
    - School classes.

UNIT 10 Public Speaking

- Job interviews.

2. **Purposes**

    1) A fast and effective method of
        - Exchanging ideas.
        - Outlining a plan or a research project.
        - Explaining a problem and rendering a solution.

    2) A demonstration of
        - Skills and abilities in public speaking.
        - Knowledge of a given area.

3. **Considerations Before Preparing a Presentation**

    1) The audience.
        - A general audience.
        - Specialists.
        - Your peers.

    2) Time allotted.

    3) Purpose of the presentation.

4. **Organization**

    1) Write the manuscript.
        - Start with "What was the problem?"
        - End with "What is the solution?"

    2) Trim down some parts.

    3) Stick to your most important point.

5. **Format of Presentations**
    - Greeting.
    - Self-introduction.
    - Aim of the presentation.
    - Outline of the presentation.
    - Main parts.
    - Summary and conclusion.
    - Inviting questions.

6. **Important Elements in an Oral Presentation**

    1) Rate
        - The optimal rate is about 100 words per minute.

- Use pauses.
- Repeat critical information.

2) Opening
- Catch the interest and attention of the audience.
- Avoid trite filler phrases.
- Avoid technical jargon.

3) Transitions
- Link between successive elements of the talk.
- Plan carefully.
- Be smooth and logical.
- Be clear to the audience.

4) Conclusion
- Summarize the main concepts.
- Summarize how your work relates to issues you've raised.
- Aim: to achieve high retention of this final information.
- Signal: "In summary, ..."

5) Length
- Short presentations: within 10 minutes.
- Symposium presentations: within 20 minutes.
- A seminar: about one hour.
- Fit the allotted time.

7. Advice on Delivery

- Speak loudly and clearly.
- Avoid speaking too fast.
- Do not mumble.
- Avoid repeatedly saying "um" or "you know".
- Vary the pitch and speed.
- Establish eye contact.
- Smile occasionally.

8. Tips for Preparation

- Rehearse.
- Video-record your speech.

UNIT 10 Public Speaking

- Watch the video critically.
- Modify and improve your speech.

Part 2 Panel Discussion

1. **Definition**
   1) Participants: a group of specialists.
   2) Different purposes:
      - To solve the problem.
      - To exchange ideas.
      - To express agreement and disagreement.

2. **Moderator**
   1) Reasons for setting a moderator:
      - To ensure a successful discussion.
      - To facilitate the discussion.
   2) The duty of a moderator:
      - To make sure the members of the discussion group stay focused on the topic.
      - To make sure each speaker finishes his/her presentation in the allocated time.
   3) Basic requirements of a moderator:
      - To understand the subject matter.
      - To know a bit about each panelist.
      - To have an innate sense of pacing.
      - To have a smooth approach of weaving in questions.
      - Not to flaunt his/her expertise and be too distracting.
   4) Three things a moderator should pay attention to:
      - Is anyone on the panel dominating the discussion?
        - Call for or direct some questions to other panelists.
        - Remind panelists of the time constraints.
      - Has someone on the panel not spoken much?
        - Direct a question to him or her.
      - Has the discussion seemingly taken a turn down a long and unproductive track?
        - Break in politely and redirect the conversation.

3. **Dos and Don'ts in a Discussion**

   1) Stay on topic.
   - Bad etiquette: to raise questions that are not related to the subject of discussion.
   - Consequence: wasting time or preventing the group from achieving its goal.
   - Make sure that any questions you ask or statements you make are related to the topic.

   2) Speak clearly and concisely.

   3) Speak audibly.

   4) Show respect to all members of the group.
   - Show mutual respect.
   - Avoid conflict.

   5) Never attack the idea of someone else.
   - Wait and state your ideas politely.
   - Bad etiquette:
     - "That idea will never work."
     - "Your idea doesn't make any sense."
   - Good alternatives:
     - "Those are interesting ideas, but I'm more concerned about…"
     - "I see your point, but there are a number of problems that may arise."

   6) Avoid interrupting other members when they are speaking.
   - Try to interject as politely as you can.
   - Raise your hands.

Part 3 Questions and Answers

1. **The Question-and-Answer Session**

   1) This is a vital aspect of engagement in your presentation.

   2) Advantages:
   - Show the audience's interest.
   - Clarify and reinforce key messages.
   - Exchange and share insights.
   - Receive valuable suggestions.

2. **Notice in Advance**
   - Let people know early that there will be a question-and-answer session.

- Encourage people to think of questions during the presentation.

3. **Be Prepared**

   1) Work through all of your material.

   2) Note down all the possible questions.
   - Collect pertinent background information.
   - Write down the answers.
   - Be familiar with the questions and answers.

4. **Prime the Pump When Nobody Asks a Question**
   - "A question I'm often asked is…"
   - Motivate audience members to ask questions.

5. **Repeat or Restate the Question**
   - It makes sure you understand the question.
   - It gives you a chance to evaluate the question and think of an answer.
   - It assures that the audience can hear the question since you are facing them.

6. **Be Brief**
   - Be brief, concise and straight to the point.
   - Give simple but informative answers.

7. **Credit the Person for Asking the Question**

8. **Be Honest and Straightforward when You Don't Know the Answer**
   - Don't guess.
   - Apologize by saying "I'm sorry. I don't happen to know the answer to that question, but I'll be happy to check into it for you."
   - Direct the question to an expert or someone from the audience.

9. **Respond to Difficult Questions**

   When the questioner is hostile:
   - Stay cool and polite.
   - Thank the person for his/her question.
   - Reply in a calm and collected tone.

10. **Maintain Control**

    1) If someone tries to dominate the question-and-answer session or asks an irrelevant question, remind or stop him/her politely.

2) The golden rules:
- Be polite to the audience.
- Stay calm.
- Never lose your temper.

11. **Conclude Strongly**
- End the session confidently.
- Plan beforehand.
- Stick to the allocated time.
- Have a closing statement or strategy at hand.

Part 4 Essentials for a Chinese

The following public speaking essentials for Chinese students aim to reduce anxiety that can interfere with giving presentations or speeches.

1) Practice.
- Talk about what you know: Choose a topic for your speech or presentation that you know a lot about and love.
- Concentrate on your message: Concentrate on the main message of your speech or presentation and make it your goal to deliver that message.
- Grab the audience's attention: Start with an interesting fact or a story that relates to your topic.
- Have one main message: Tie different parts of your talk to the main theme to support your overall message.

2) Prepare.
- Visit the room: Take the time to visit the room in advance and get used to standing at the front of the room.
- Rack up experience: Volunteer to speak as often as possible. Build up confidence with every public speaking experience.
- Observe other speakers: Take the time to watch other speakers who are good at what they do. Practice imitating their style and confidence.
- Organize your talk: Structure your talk with an introduction, a body, and a conclusion, so that the audience know what to expect.

UNIT 10 Public Speaking

3) Manage your anxiety.
   - Tell someone about your anxiety: Meet with your teacher or professor and describe your public speaking fears. Or share your fears with your parents, a teacher, or a guidance counselor.
   - Visualize confidence: Visualize yourself confidently delivering your speech. Imagine feeling free of anxiety and engaging the audience.
4) Be confident.
   - Develop your own style: Work on developing your own personal style as a public speaker. Integrate your own personality into your speaking style.
   - Vary your tone, volume, and speed: Vary the pitch (high vs. low), volume (loud vs. soft), and speed (fast vs. slow) of your words.
5) Watch for feedback and adapt to it.
   - Keep the focus on the audience.
   - Gauge their reactions, adjust your message, and stay flexible.

Section III Let's Do It!

Activity 1 Being Non-offensive

Being non-offensive means that you avoid expressions and actions that may exclude, marginalize, or offend a particular group of people. It promotes equality by demonstrating an understanding that all people and groups are valuable to society regardless of race, culture, religion, gender, or sexual orientation. Being non-offensive, sometimes referred to as being politically correct, is very important when delivering a speech. Now try to figure out the non-offensive way of saying the following terms:

- bald: _____
- blind: _____
- broken home: _____
- censorship: _____
- chairman: _____
- clumsy: _____

- deaf: _____
- fat: _____
- fireman: _____
- gang: _____
- garbage man: _____
- homeless: _____
- immigrant: _____
- insane people: _____
- learning disability: _____
- mankind: _____
- policeman/policewoman: _____
- postman: _____
- short: _____
- steward/stewardess: _____
- stupid: _____
- the elderly: _____
- used books: _____

Activity 2   Describing a Famous Person

Prepare a short presentation with the title "A Famous Person That I Admire". Include all the necessary elements in your presentation.

You should include:
- who the person is and where he/she lives;
- what the person does;
- what you admire about this person;
- what you think people can learn from this person.

Activity 3   Starting a Presentation

A strong and engaging opening is a must for a successful presentation. Everything that follows can build from the opening outline you present to your audience. Read the following guidelines for starting a presentation and come up with your own sentences.

UNIT 10 Public Speaking

Introduction Outline:

1) Introduce Yourself and Welcome Everyone

   The self-introduction is your opportunity to make a good first impression. Be sure to open with a warm welcome and use language that is familiar and natural. Think of a few different expressions you can use to start your presentation, based on your audience:

   - If you're presenting to coworkers who may have already known you:

   _____
   _____

   - If you're presenting to people you've never met:

   _____
   _____

2) State the Purpose of Your Presentation

   Now that your audience knows who you are and your qualifications, you can state the purpose of your presentation. This is where you clarify to your audience what you'll be talking about.

   _____
   _____

3) A Short Overview of the Presentation

   The final step to start your presentation is to give a short overview of what you'll be presenting. It helps you organize your thoughts and give a sense of order. Also, it lets the audience know why they're listening to you. This is what you'll use to grab their attention, and help them stay focused throughout the presentation.

   _____
   _____

Activity 4 Analyzing Strategies Used to Handle Hostile Questions

When delivering a presentation, sometimes someone in the audience may contradict, criticize, or attack you or your idea. So response strategies are important. Read the following responses to hostile questions and analyze the strategies that have been used.

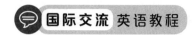

1) "It sounds like your main concern is with the methodology. Is that correct?"
2) "Thank you for your question. (Brief Pause) There are a few ways I could respond. (Brief Pause) Let me say this..."
3) When you have finished your response, say, "Thank you for your question. Does anyone else have a question?"
4) Question: "Why are you demanding that we submit these forms with an approval signature? I think that's totally unreasonable."
   Response: "Why do we think the forms should have an approval signature? Well, first of all, the approval signature allows us to..."
5) Simple comment: "No, I don't think that's the case." or "No elaboration is necessary."
6) "It sounds as though you've been through some difficult delays with this supplier." or "I don't blame you for feeling as you do, given the situation you describe. I'm just glad that has been the exception rather than the rule in working with this audit group."
7) "My experience has been different. Based on X, Y, and Z, it's my opinion that ABC approach will work in our situation."
8) "I have to confess: I do not know how to properly answer your question right now. But please do give me your contact information and I will be happy to communicate the answer to your question once I have researched it."

Activity 5   How to Gracefully Interrupt a Dominant Panelist

A moderator needs to be aware whether anyone on the panel is dominating the discussion or talks for too long. Imagine you are a moderator, what phrases can you use to intervene when you need to, and direct some questions to other panelists? Write them down.

1) _____
2) _____
3) _____
4) _____
5) _____
6) _____
7) _____

UNIT 10 Public Speaking

Activity 6 Appreciating an Effective Speech

You are going to watch a speech entitled "Chess Board" given by Tughluk, a student from Tsinghua University.

Take notes while watching. After watching it, work in a group, pool your ideas, and:

- summarize the main idea in the speech;
- lay out the structure of this speech and work out a mind map;
- explain why this speech is convincing and impressive.

Section IV Tool Box

1. Useful Words and Expressions

   1) Giving an Opinion / Expressing an Opinion
      - In my opinion / In my view...
      - My view is that / My point of view is that...
      - I reckon / I feel / Personally speaking...
      - As far as I am concerned...
      - It seems to me that...
      - Well, I would say...
      - I would like to point out...
      - If you want my opinion...
      - The way I look at it...
      - As I see it...
      - The point I am trying to make is...
      - I think/believe that...
      - I suppose/presume/would say...
      - I think most people would agree that...
      - I believe it is hard to deny that...
      - I strongly believe that...
      - I think none would deny that...

2) Agreeing with an Opinion
- I quite agree...
- I completely agree that...
- Yes, indeed...
- I could not agree more...
- I entirely/totally agree with you on that...
- That's exactly how I see it...
- That's exactly what I think/believe...
- Precisely/Exactly/Certainly/Definitely.
- You are quite right about...
- You have just read my mind...
- Yes, that's obvious...

3) Disagreeing with an Opinion
- I possess a different view...
- I must disagree with the view that...
- I am afraid I believe/see it otherwise...
- This might be true in some context but...
- I am inclined to oppose the view that...
- I am afraid I disagree...
- Yes, perhaps, but...
- Well, it depends...
- I see what you mean, but this is not the whole story...
- Yes, but there is also another aspect to consider...
- I don't quite agree that...
- Well, that's one way to look at that, but...
- I am not quite so sure that...

4) Asking for Help / Asking to Repeat Something / Asking for an Explanation
- I am not sure what you meant by...
- Could you please say that in other words?
- Could you please repeat the question?
- Do you mean...?
- I am sorry. Could you please repeat that?
- I beg your pardon...

- Could you please explain it to me in another way?
- I did not quite get that. Did you mean...?

5) Buying Some Time / Stalling for Time
- That's an interesting/difficult/tough question...
- I have never really thought about it, but...
- I don't know much about it, but...
- I have not given enough thought on that...
- Well, not sure where should I start...

6) Interrupting
- Sorry to interrupt...
- If I may interrupt...

7) Drawing the Conclusion / Ending a Discussion
- In summary, I can say that...
- So, that's why I think that...
- Anyway, that's why...

2. Useful Sentences

1) Giving an Opinion / Expressing an Opinion
- In my opinion, we should encourage children to have more outdoor activities than playing computer games.
- Personally speaking, the trend has changed to a great extent than that of our forefathers' era.

2) Agreeing with an Opinion
- I quite agree that music choice by the young generation is often considered tasteless by the senior citizens.
- Yes, indeed, it is our responsibility to save the endangered species.

3) Disagreeing with an Opinion
- I am afraid I believe otherwise and feel that ordinary citizens like us have a much greater role here.
- Yes, perhaps, but my experience has taught me that I should plan beforehand rather than rushing it.

4) Asking for Help / Asking to Repeat Something / Asking for an Explanation
- I beg your pardon; I could not catch the last sentence.
- I did not quite get that. Did you mean what social changes occurred during

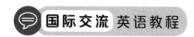

the past two decades?

5) Buying Some Time / Stalling for Time
   - That's an interesting question and I would like to thank you for asking me this. I believe that waste recycling is not a choice but a mandatory task.
   - I don't know much about it but from my personal experience, I can say that we should focus on more pressing issues rather than wasting money on things that have yet to bring any positive output.
   - I have not given enough thought on that but I feel the trend is not a good one.

6) Interrupting
   - Sorry to interrupt but I would like to say that I come from a city which has better facilities than the one you mentioned just now.
   - If I may interrupt, I would like to finish by saying that this is what most of the ordinary citizens believe about our legislative system.

7) Drawing the Conclusion / Ending a Discussion
   - Anyway, that's why we are the supreme beings and we should act accordingly.
   - In summary, I can say that we still have to monitor this closely before taking any whimsical decision.

Section V Do You Know?

Supplementary Readings

Read the following three passages and find out more about public speaking. The answers to the questions at the beginning of each passage can be found through reading.

Passage 1 How to Introduce Yourself Before a Presentation

Questions:
- Why is it important to introduce yourself in a presentation?

UNIT 10 Public Speaking

♦ Is it enough just to list your credentials or job title? Why or why not?
♦ How would you transition from the introduction to your content?

Introducing yourself in a presentation is more than just saying your name. It's an opportunity for you to share relevant details about yourself and connect with your audience. It also sets the tone for the rest of the talk. How you introduce yourself will influence how your audience receives the message you want to get across. Make your next introduction flawless by presenting the most engaging information about yourself. Be sure to prepare the introduction in advance and start with an attention-grabbing technique to engage the audience.

State Your Name Clearly

You want the audience to remember who you are, so don't mumble or rush out your name. Speak loudly and confidently, and make sure you enunciate every syllable.

If you have a name that is unusual or difficult to pronounce, you may want to add a small remark to help your audience remember it. For example, you can say "My name is Jacob Misen, like 'risen' but with an M".

Communicate Your Contribution to Get the Audience Excited

Think about how you will help your audience and briefly communicate with them, rather than just listing your credentials or job titles. Your basic credentials will probably be listed on the presentation slide, anyway. Ask yourself what special skills and experience you have that would interest your audience and introduce yourself with those.

If you are VP of Marketing at a large company, it can actually be much more effective to say something like "I have more than a decade of experience using Facebook marketing ads to target clients in the dance industry," rather than simply stating your job title.

Leave Extra Details on a Handout or PowerPoint Slide

If there are other details about yourself that are interesting and relevant to the presentation, you don't have to list them all in your introduction. Instead, add them to your handout or PowerPoint slide. Your audience can read them there if they want.

You can also specifically refer your audience to the handout or PowerPoint slide

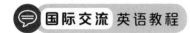

for more information. For example, if you want to let them know that you have articles in many international newspapers but you don't want to list them all out, simply say "I've written for a number of internationally recognized news organizations. You can find the full list on the first page of my handout."

Save Some Relevant Details About Yourself for Later in the Presentation

You don't have to give the audience everything about yourself right away. Stick to the most interesting and relevant information. If you have other interesting personal details you want to share, you can add them in other parts of the presentation.

For example, you could say "When I designed a website for Richard Branson last year..." to inform your audience that you have an impressive resumé, instead of listing it all for them in your introduction.

Plan a Smooth Transition from the Introduction to Your Content

Once you've got a great introduction, it's important you seamlessly and effectively transition into the meat of your presentation. Having a planned transition will also help you maintain your confidence because you'll know exactly where you are going and how to get there.

Try concluding your introduction by mentioning a client or project you were working on that directly relates to the topic of your presentation. For example, "I've had the pleasure of working with NXP Semiconductors for the past three years. Just last week we encountered a problem with our logistical database..." and then lead into your presentation about a new software that will solve everyone's logistical hiccups.

Passage 2 How to Start a Presentation Strong by Leveraging Unpredictability

Questions:
- Why is unpredictability more engaging?
- How can we decide on the way to incorporate unpredictability at the start of a presentation?

UNIT 10 Public Speaking

> ♦ Why do we say "one of the most powerful ways to start a presentation is to stimulate curiosity"?
> ♦ If you want to ask questions at the beginning of your presentation, what are the features of these questions?

Starting a presentation strong means being unpredictable. Research shows that when we know what to expect from a cue, we don't pay attention to what happens after the cue. But when we don't know what to expect, we pay more attention. That's why we love movies with a twist: The unpredictability engages us more deeply.

How can you incorporate unpredictability at the start of a presentation? There are several ways to achieve this. The choice will depend on your topic, the circumstances, and your presentation style. The techniques below guide us on how to start a presentation strong.

Make a Bold Claim

Everyone knows the "I Have a Dream" speech of Martin Luther King, Jr. The speech doesn't begin with "I have a dream." That's the climax. The speech starts like this: "I am happy to join with you today in what will go down in history as the greatest demonstration for freedom in the history of our nation."

The above claim may seem "normal" to us today. We already know the events of history. But can you imagine what it must have been like hearing that claim on that very day? Bold, to say the least. Could anyone in the audience help but pay attention after that?

If you're confident your presentation will make a measurable and immediate impact on your audience, don't save that claim for the end. State it at the beginning and state it with confidence. When your audience understands the gains, they can't help but pay attention to your every word.

Contradict Expectations

Let's look at another interesting way to start a presentation. Consider contradicting expectations. This is a classic application of the unpredictability principle.

Start with a claim that contradicts what people expect. That will make them sit up

and pay attention. Then use the attention you've earned to ease into your topic.

Sir Ken Robinson does this marvelously in the most-watched Ted Talk of all time. Coming onto the stage after all the other speakers, Robinson says: "It's been great, hasn't it? I've been blown away by the whole thing. In fact, I'm leaving."

You can hear in the way the audience laughs that this statement catches them by surprise. And the speaker uses that surprise to lunge into the topic.

Pamela Meyer achieves similar results through a slightly different technique. Meyer begins a presentation on how to spot a liar by accusing the audience of being liars themselves! "Okay, I don't want to alarm anybody in this room, but it's just come to my attention that the person to your right is a liar! Also, the person to your left is a liar."

The audience laughs. They weren't expecting to be called liars. But the contrarian claim isn't off-putting; it's captivating. "Why are we all liars?" they want to know, and now they're paying attention.

Stimulate Curiosity

One of the most powerful ways to start a presentation is to stimulate curiosity. The human brain relishes curiosity. In fact, research has shown that curiosity prepares the brain for better learning. And that's good news for your presentation.

Why? Because once our curiosity is piqued, we want to know the answer. We must solve the puzzle. So, we pay attention to looking for the right clues. It's simply the way we were built to think and operate.

So how can you stimulate curiosity at the beginning of your presentation? You could announce that you've got a secret to confess, like Dan Pink does in a famous Ted Talk: "I need to make a confession, at the outset here. A little over 20 years ago, I did something that I regret. Something that I am not particularly proud of. Something that in many ways I wished no one would ever know, but that here I feel kind of obliged to reveal. In the late 1980s, in a moment of youthful indiscretion, I went to law school."

The announcement of this confession piques our curiosity. What's the secret? And the contents of the confession heighten it. Why is going to law school such an embarrassing confession? We must solve this puzzle! And so, there's no option but to pay close attention to every word to find out!

Ask Questions

A simple yet effective approach to start a presentation that grips attention is to ask a question. Nothing is more unexpected than a speaker beginning a presentation with questions. Isn't the speaker supposed to answer our questions?

But these questions are rhetorical. They're not meant to be answered with a simple "yes" or "no". They intend to plant the seed of an idea into our heads. The speaker can then focus our attention on that idea throughout the presentation.

Simon Sinek does this in a talk on how great leaders inspire action. Sinek begins by asking the audience: "How do you explain when things don't go as we assumed? Or better, how do you explain when others are able to achieve things that seem to defy all of the assumptions? For example, why is Apple so innovative? [...] Why is it that Martin Luther King led the civil rights movement?"

By this point, we're all sitting there scratching our chins going: "Huh, how do they do that?" So, we perk our ears and pay attention.

Spin a Surprising Story

One of the most gripping ways to start a presentation is to tell a compelling story, especially a surprising one.

The story is not just an entrainment mechanism, but a survival mechanism humans have developed and refined over thousands of years. That means as humans, we're naturally wired to pay attention to stories.

And one of the best ways to start your presentation strong is by telling a story. It can be a story about something that happened to you. Or something you heard about. Either way, it should relate to your topic and why you're giving your presentation.

That's how Brené Brown opens a now-famous Ted Talk about vulnerability. Brown relates the funny story of working with an event planner who didn't know how to classify Brown for an event. Turns out, Brown didn't know, either!

Should Brown be called a researcher (which sounds boring) or a storyteller (which sounded something like a magic pixie to Brené Brown at the time)? In the end, Brown calls herself a researcher-storyteller.

The story delights and intrigues: What's a researcher-storyteller? And how does researcher tell a story? We pay attention to find out.

Passage 3 How to Prepare Notes for Public Speaking

Questions:
- What is the first recommendation given in this passage?
- When making notes, why are brief phrases better than full sentences?
- Is it suggested to used double-sided notes? Why or why not?

Imagine you have a big presentation next week and you're unsure what to bring with you on stage. You know your subject matter but are afraid of losing your place halfway through the speech. At the same time, you don't want to write the speech out and memorize it because you're afraid it will sound inauthentic.

One of the questions I get asked most often is: What type of notes should I bring to my presentation: bullet points, a script, or nothing at all?

First and foremost, I do not recommend memorizing your speech word-for-word; when you do that, you spend more time trying to recall the next phrase than you do connecting with your audience. For that same reason, I don't recommend using a script of your speech: It's difficult to make a connection with the audience if your eye contact, voice, and energy are focused on looking down at your words.

Most of the time, it's perfectly fine to bring bullet points with you to a speech or presentation. Because many people fear forgetting their main messages, having the bullet points nearby can reduce speech anxiety. You are able to relax and focus on your message; then, if you need to remind yourself of the next point, you can glance down at the bullet points to find your place.

There are times when it is acceptable to bring the script of the entire speech with you to the presentation, such as during a formal occasion when you had limited time to prepare or a legal proceeding in which every word matters. However, most of the time, simply bring bullets. Here are some tips for using bullet points:

Write Brief Phrases Instead of Full Sentences

When you glance down at your notes, it's easier to find your place if you look for a phrase rather than a full sentence. Phrases also help you speak conversationally instead of reading from a script. If the story in your speech is about an experience in Miami, write "MIAMI" instead of writing out, "Let me tell you about some work we're doing in Miami, Florida."

Use Lots of White Space

Don't try to cram all of your bullets onto one page; include spaces between points so you can easily find your place.

Print Single-Sided Pages

Using single-sided paper helps you easily move from one page to the next, while double-sided notes require you to flip the paper back and forth which can confuse you. Write page numbers at the top of each page in case they fall out of order before (or during) the speech.

Use Large Font

Print or write your bullets in large font so you don't have to squint at a piece of paper—it will be quicker and more seamless to glance down if you can easily read the words.

Practice the Speech with the Bullet Points in Front of You

Speaking from bullet points takes practice as you'll need to add in transitions and descriptions on your own. Make time to practice giving the speech with the bullet points so you familiarize yourself with where the words fall on the paper.

During the Speech, Rest the Notes on a Lectern or Table

Try not to hold them in your hand, otherwise they may reveal your shaky hands or you may subconsciously start to play with the paper. Also, feel free to move around the stage, away from the lectern. It creates a better connection with your audience and you can always walk back to your notes when you need them.

Don't Apologize for Looking Down

It's natural for us to look down and find our place; it's not a fault or mistake. Simply pause, nod thoughtfully, look down, and keep going. The more comfortable you are, the more comfortable the audience will be.

Unless you're giving a TED talk, it's OK to use some form of bullet points—and bullets are always preferable to a script. It does take extra time to prepare, but it leads to a more authentic and more engaging speech for all involved.

There are two versions of every speech: the version you write and the version you deliver. They are rarely the same, and that's OK as it keeps your speech fresh and authentic.

Take the time to create bullet points that remind you of your main points, practice using those notes, and then focus on your message and your motivation. The more comfortable you are with your message and the more prepared you are when you walk on stage, the more powerful your speech will be.

UNIT 11

Telephone Etiquette

Learning Objectives

After learning this unit, you will be able to:
- understand the protocol of international communication in making and answering phone calls;
- compare the cultural differences in terms of etiquette of telephoning;
- learn to speak on the phone properly and communicate successfully in international communication;
- comprehend the value of mutual respect and courtesy in international communication.

Section I Warm-Up

1. How do we make phone calls in China? Do we speak differently when calling different people for different purposes? Write down as much Chinese phone etiquette as you can.

   _____
   _____
   _____
   _____
   _____

2. Write down as many situations as you can for making phone calls when you are abroad.

   _____
   _____
   _____
   _____
   _____

Section II Points to Remember

There are important points to remember and some rules to follow in present-day international communication. The following is a summary of the basics in regard to making and answering phone calls. Referring to these points constantly may help you communicate with international friends more effectively and politely.

Part 1 Why Is Telephoning Such an Important Skill for International Communication?

- Usually a phone call is the first contact that a person has with a company.
- The way you answer and make telephone calls will create a first impression about

UNIT 11 Telephone Etiquette

you and your company based on efficiency, communication skills, friendliness and expertise.

Part 2   Types of Telephones

There are basically three types of telephones: landlines, mobile phones or cell phones and online phones.

1) A landline is a traditional telephone used in homes and offices. It has a receiver, sometimes a dial, or a keypad with keys and buttons. Sometimes there is an answering machine connected to the landline to record messages.
   - With a landline you can make local calls and long-distance calls.
   - To make a long-distance call you need an area code. IDD refers to International Direct Dialing, consisting of country code plus area code plus telephone number.
   - Collect calls are the calls that the recipient must pay for the bill.
   - When you make a telephone call, you need a telephone directory and telephone bills are usually paid monthly.
2) Mobile phones or cell phones are usually used for private purposes.
3) Some people also use online phones to make international calls for free.

Part 3   Answering the Telephone

1. Four Steps
   - Hear the telephone ring.
   - Lift the receiver or press/slide the start/listening key.
   - Answer the phone call with a "Hello?"
   - Speak and then hang up the phone with a "Goodbye" or by pressing/sliding the stop key.

2. The Important Elements in a Telephone Message
   - Who called?
   - Whom to?
   - What is the matter concerned?
   - Why?

- Where?
- When?
- And other important messages.

3. **Basic Telephone Etiquette**
   - Answer the telephone on the third ring.
   - Greet the caller and identify yourself briefly and clearly.
   - Be prepared before you answer the phone.
   - Be an active listener and respond.
   - Return phone calls promptly.
   - Check your messages frequently. Ask the caller to slow down or repeat if necessary.
   - Do not speak too fast.
   - Thank the caller before saying goodbye and hang up.

Part 4　Making Telephone Calls

1. **Preparations for Making a Call**
   - Make a list of things you need to say.
   - Confirm the schedule so that you call at a proper time.
   - Check a telephone directory: if necessary.
   - Have a telephone message form or some paper and a pen.

2. **Telephone Etiquette**
   - Be prepared before you make the telephone call.
   - Greet the person answering the phone and identify yourself briefly and clearly.
   - Pronounce your name clearly.
   - Slow down when you are giving your telephone number.
   - Give the name of your institution or company and your title, and say why you are calling.
   - Let the person answering the phone know when to call you back.
   - Do not hang up without saying thank-you and goodbye.

Part 5　Essentials for a Chinese

The following are some additional telephone etiquette to practice when you are in

UNIT 11 Telephone Etiquette

international communication scenarios:

- Always identify yourself every time you call.
- Address the person that you are talking to by name.
- Watch your tone. Speak clearly and slowly so that the other person understands.
- Make sure you know what you want to say before you make a call.
- If you have any questions, just ask.
- Ask for clarity.
- Repeat important information.
- Don't waste other people's time.
- Just get right to the point.
- Don't call late at night or on weekends.
- When you are on the phone, don't be silent. Give the other person full attention.
- Don't sound anxious, aggressive or pushy.
- Don't talk too much. Let the other person talk.
- Don't hang up on the other person. If you do this, call back right away.
- You need to make sure that you are saying exactly what you want to say.
- Avoid dead silences or long pauses in a conversation. When having a conversation, don't stop to think about what you want to say.
- When leaving a message, leave your name as well as your phone number. Make sure you speak slowly and clearly. Also, mention why you are calling. And, if you need the person to call you back, suggest an appropriate time.
- Know the appropriate time to call. It's better to call between nine and eleven in the morning. Regular business hours are Monday to Friday from 9 am to 5 pm. If it is a personal call, call between 9 am and 9 pm If the other person has small children, maybe eight o'clock in the evening is the latest time to call.
- All through the phone call, you should always be polite and courteous to the other person.
- At the end of the call, say thank-you and end it by saying goodbye.

And you can add more...

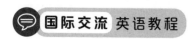

Section III Let's Do It!

Activity 1 Listening to a Telephone Conversation

1. Suppose you are working in your supervisor's office and suddenly the telephone rings. If the caller wants to speak to your supervisor who is not in, what are you going to do? Take notes and fill in the blanks of this telephone conversation.

   A: Hello, this is Harbin Institute of Technology. Department of Automation. _____?

   B: Hello, my name is Gerard Edwards and I'm calling from Vancouver, Canada. _____ Professor Gao, please?

   A: I'm sorry Professor Gao is not here at the moment. _____ _____?

   B: Yes, thank you. I'm attending a conference _____ and I'm calling to inform you about my flight information.

   A: Could you spell your name please?

   B: Certainly. G-E-R-A-R-D E-D-W-A-R-D-S. That is G-E-R-A-R-D E-D-W-A-R-D-S, Gerard Edwards.

   A: Gerard Edwards, _____. Thank you and your message, Professor Edwards.

   B: I'm arriving in Harbin next Wednesday on the 20th on CZ6267.

   A: Ok Professor Edwards, _____. You are arriving on CZ6267 next Wednesday, the 20th of May, right?

   B: Yes, _____. Please also inform Professor Gao that I will send him the title of my speech via email later today.

   A: _____, Professor Edwards. Is there anything else I can help with?

   B: No, thank you. _____.

   A: _____, Professor Edwards.

   B: You are welcome. Goodbye.

222

UNIT 11 Telephone Etiquette

2. Answer the following questions based on the telephone conversation.
    1) Who called?
    2) Whom did the caller want to speak to?
    3) What information did the caller give?
    4) What do you think of the way the call is answered? Why?

Activity 2 Making a Call in English

Read the following scenario descriptions and pick your role. Imagine you and your partner both are on the phone and cannot see each other's facial expressions. After you have finished the call, switch your roles and do it the second time.

The following cues may help you:

	Student A's Cue Card	Student B's Cue Card
Scenarios	You are an international student from China who has just arrived in a famous university. Call your supervisor and arrange to see him/her.	You are an officer working in the International Department of a famous university. You are responsible for supervising a group of international students. Make sure you meet them when they arrive at your university and give them your contact information.
Language Tips	• Hello. • May I speak to XXX? • I am XXX, from XXX.	• Hello. • This is the International Department. • May I help you?
	• I'd like to make an appointment to meet you and discuss with you about my study plan. • Yes, I can. Where shall we meet? • I think I can find it. • Thank you so much. • Goodbye.	• This is XXX speaking. • Sure. • Can you make it at XXX (time) on XXX (day of the week)? • How about XXX? • Thanks for calling and see you then.

Activity 3 Describing Your First Mobile Phone

My First Mobile Phone

Time	Brand	Given by	Features	Uses

Fill in the table first. Tell your partner about the first mobile phone you have ever had. The following questions may help you remember. Then use those questions to ask about your partner's first mobile phone.

- When did you have it?
- What was it for?
- Who gave it to you?
- What was its brand?
- Was it new? Expensive? Did you like it?
- What did you use it for?
- How long have you had it?
- Do you still have it?
- What happened to it?

Activity 4 A Discussion on Mobile Phone Etiquette

Discuss in groups what people should know when using their mobile phones properly in public, with friends, and on international communication occasions. List at least three Dos and Don'ts.

Dos	Don'ts
e.g., Put the phone on silent mode while in class.	e.g., Don't put the phone on the table while having dinner.

UNIT 11 Telephone Etiquette

Activity 5   Calling to Say Thank-You

Suppose that you have completed your study and want to call your supervisor/professor before you leave to say thank-you and make an appointment to see him/her.

Your partner will answer your call as the supervisor/professor. Exchange your roles after one round of role-play. Use your real mobile phone to make a call and don't look at each other during the conversation. Listen carefully and speak naturally. Then volunteer to act it out in front of the class.

Section IV   Tool Box

1. **Useful Words and Expressions**
   - 手机 mobile/cell phone
   - 智能手机 smart phone
   - 手机用户 mobile phone user/subscriber
   - 手机入网费 initiation charges for mobile phone / mobile access fee
   - 手机实名制 mobile phone identification policy
   - 全球定位系统 GPS (Global Positioning System)
   - 短信服务 SMS (Short Message Service)
   - 客户身份识别卡 SIM (Subscriber Identity Module)
   - 全球移动通信系统 GSM (Global System For Mobile Communications)
   - 储值卡 pre-paid phone card
   - 按键 keypad
   - 手机充电 cellular phone recharging
   - 手机流量 data
   - 用过的手机流量 data usage
   - 包月手机流量 data plan
   - 发帖 share/post
   - 点赞 like
   - 转发 forward
   - 收藏 favorite
   - 充值 top up

- 表情符号 emoji
- 同步 sync
- 关注 follow
- 取消关注 unfollow
- 联系人，通讯录 contacts
- 漫游 roaming service
- 短信 short message / text message
- 手机铃音 mobile phone ringtone
- 振动 vibrate
- 待机模式 standby mode
- 菜单模式 list view / grid view
- 快捷图标 short-cut icon
- 自动重拨 automatic redial
- 语音拨号 voice dial
- 呼出通话 outgoing call
- 被叫通话 incoming call
- 近来的呼叫 recent call
- 未接电话 missed call
- 已接电话 received call
- 不在服务区 out of reach

2. **Useful Sentences**

　1) Identifying Your Company
- Hello. Engineering Department. Can I help you?
- Good morning. International Exchange Centre.

　2) Identifying Yourself
- This is Jennifer. / Jennifer speaking. / Jennifer here.

　3) Identifying the Caller
- Who's calling, please? / Who's that speaking? / May I ask who's calling?
- I'm sorry, I didn't catch your name.

　4) Asking for Connection
- I'd like to speak to the Physics Department.
- Could you put me through to the Engineering Department?
- Could I have extension 244, please?

UNIT 11 Telephone Etiquette

- Could I speak to someone in the English Department?

5) Explaining the Purpose
   - I'm calling about...
   - The reason I'm calling is...
   - It's about...
   - It's in connection with...

6) Asking About the Purpose
   - Could you tell me what it's about?
   - What's it in connection with?

7) Making the Connection
   - Just a moment.
   - I'm putting you through.

Section V Do You Know?

Supplementary Readings

Read the following three passages and find out more about telephone etiquette. The answers to the questions at the beginning of each passage can be found through reading.

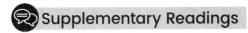

Passage 1 Ten Reasons for Learning Telephone Skills

> Questions:
> ♦ Why should we know the reasons for learning telephone skills?
> ♦ What do we do that may exceed customer's expectations?
> ♦ How should we speak if the caller is upset?

Effective telephone communication is vital to the success of your business. Interacting with customers can be a frustrating experience if you don't know the proper telephone etiquette. With a smile in your voice and with the right techniques, however, these interactions can be enjoyable and profitable. Learning these skills is easy when you know why they are important.

Keep Customers

Good telephone skills retain customers. People are more likely to do business with you again if your telephone conversations with them are pleasant and helpful. If you provide a frustrating telephone experience, customers are more likely to do business elsewhere.

Gain New Customers

Word of mouth is a powerful form of advertising for your business. If your customers feel that you care about their needs, they will tell their friends about your business; however, they will also tell their friends if they don't feel valued, and their bad experience will cost you new customers.

Exceed Expectations

You can easily exceed your customer's expectations with good telephone skills. Customers often call with problems; they expect to pick a fight. You will catch your customers off guard when you are pleasant, calm and helpful and will create a pleasant impression on behalf of your company.

Avoid Repeat Calls

If you hate talking on the phone, the best thing to do is to avoid repeat calls. Effective listening and problem-solving skills ensure that your customers don't have to call repeatedly to get issues resolved. Fewer phone calls mean more time for you to spend on other important aspects of your business.

Create a Positive Atmosphere

A positive opening sets the stage for a positive customer experience. A warm, inviting greeting and an enthusiastic tone tell the caller that he/she is not causing an interruption. Instead of giving him/her the impression that he/she is wasting your time, your tone can make him/her feel like he/she is the most important person to you at that moment.

Leave a Lasting Impression

Ending your call properly helps the caller feel valued and avoids miscommunication.

Quickly summarize the issues raised during the call and ask the caller if he/she needs any additional assistance. This shows your desire to make sure he/she is satisfied with your interaction. End by thanking him/her for calling to show that he/she is valued.

Diffuse Anger

Telephone skills help to calm a caller down when he/she is upset. Knowing how to use tone and empathy shows your willingness to work with the caller to solve the problem. If you speak softly and don't interrupt the caller, your interaction is likely to go more smoothly and result in a satisfactory outcome for both of you.

Become Known for Immediate Action

Callers hate delays. With effective telephone skills, you can gain a reputation for solving problems quickly. Enjoy a successful telephone interaction by learning to express your willingness to assist and your ability to meet the callers' needs quickly.

Cut Through Confusion

With effective telephone skills, you can cut through confusion and fully understand the situation. Listen without interrupting. This makes the caller feel valued and makes it easier to resolve customer complaints.

Increase Sales

Effective telephone skills put you in a better position to sell additional products to your customers. They will be more receptive to what you have to offer if you are friendly, enthusiastic and eager to solve their problems.

Passage 2 How to Communicate Efficiently on the Phone

Questions:
- How many pieces of advice are given in this passage?
- What can we do to convince the other person that we are happy to be speaking with them?
- What should we do to avoid missing what the caller is saying?

Good telephone skills always impress, and will always be highly valued.

It may come to your surprise, but even in the age of Internet and social media, businesses are still primarily being reached by phone. Therefore, working on your phone answering skills is a sensible investment of your time.

There are not many jobs that do not involve any phone calls so it is worth thinking about what you should do to improve your phone communication skills.

Be Enthusiastic and Speak Clearly

These are two of the most basic and essential skills you need when handling a call.

It is important to convince the other person that you are happy to be speaking with them. To do so, you should be taking every call with a smile and energy in your voice. You want to transmit your eagerness to help your caller, and your voice has to exude warmth, so they feel satisfied with the interaction. People do not need much to be cheered up.

Of course, enthusiasm is not everything. It is equally important to speak slowly and clearly, so callers understand what you are saying. You should develop your composure during a phone conversation and make sure you do not fire off words in someone's ears. Confidence comes with experience but, at first, you need to remember to be as calm as possible when you pick up the phone as this will slow down your speech and make it more distinguishable.

Practice, Practice, Practice!

Some smart bloke once said that "success" comes before "work" only in the dictionary. And "result" doesn't come before "practice" even there.

If you want to project dazzling phone skills, you have to train yourself (and your colleagues and employees) how to approach calls. Phone answering is just like any other skill you want to master—you have to exercise it regularly in order to get it right.

The idea of practicing is not only to get better at what you are doing, but also to establish it as some sort of a reflex you perform naturally. In the case of phone answering, you should reach a level when you do not think about having to smile or to speak slowly and clearly.

UNIT 11 Telephone Etiquette

The flawless diction and the enthusiasm in your voice can be developed through various means. You can record yourself and listen to the recordings, or you could ask friends, relatives or colleagues (pretty much anyone) for feedback. It is always good to hear someone else's opinion as they will see things differently and can provide you with ideas on how to polish your skills.

Concentrate Only on the Call

What is the one key skill you need to demonstrate when answering the phone? In truth, there probably isn't one single most important factor. Instead, it is a complex set of skills that you need.

However, I would strongly advocate paying attention to...paying attention. Yes, concentrating on a phone call is critical if you want to deliver a positive experience to the person on the other end of the line.

This is especially so if you are working in a call centre, or speaking with customers or business prospects who are effectively bringing money to your business, and therefore to you personally. You should try to isolate yourself from your surroundings as it is crucial that your caller has your full attention.

Concentrating only on the ongoing call will sharpen your senses and you will be able to focus on the matter your caller has raised. Being completely focused on the call reduces the risk of making factual errors or misinterpreting what the other person is saying. There is no need to go into detail about the possible consequences of such mistakes: I'm sure you can figure those out yourself.

Learn to Be Patient

Coupled with the advice to listen carefully to what a caller is saying, you should also remain patient and wait until the other person is finished. Interrupting is not an option.

Listening skills are hard to develop, both during phone conversations and face-to-face communication. However, you need to learn patience as this is a particularly handy skill when delivering customer service on behalf of a business. Sometimes you may have to speak with angry clients, and here you will be expected to demonstrate your listening skills and patience. Let the other person say whatever they have to say, as long as it is not abusive or threatening, and then offer the best possible solution to

their problem.

Double-Check Important Information

Sometimes, no matter how hard you listen to the caller, you may miss bits of what they are saying.

This could be due to a momentary line disruption or the person may not be speaking very clearly (perhaps they have an accent). On such occasions, it is not only acceptable but also recommended to ask them politely to repeat what they have just said. It is not uncommon to fail to grasp a name, a phone number, or other potentially significant detail during a call, so don't worry if you have to ask your caller to repeat something. It is always better to ask for clarification than to rely on something you are not entirely sure about or have completely missed.

Speaking of that, another useful tip is to always double-check important information gathered from the customer since getting every detail right can play a major role in your future relationship. For example, you certainly need to make sure you have got their name right. As far as I am concerned, there is a difference between being called Joe, Josh or John. But it is not only the name and, if you are taking an order, you should always confirm your caller's preference to avoid any misunderstanding that could result in the order being inaccurately processed.

 **Cellphone Etiquette for the Clueless**

> **Questions:**
> ♦ What is the foremost concern when we take a call?
> ♦ What are the locations where cell phones must be switched off?
> ♦ What fundamental principle of good manners should we refer to when observing cell phone etiquette?

There are very few people in this world who possess the kind of social graces intrinsic to the characters in an Austen novel. Some would argue the children of the "information revolution" lack social propriety altogether. Despite the rumors that etiquette is dead, many of us do manage to exercise a little common courtesy

UNIT 11 Telephone Etiquette

toward our fellow man. After all etiquette exists simply to make the whole society caper a little less confrontational. The introduction of wireless communication has taken social interaction to an unprecedented level. Mobile technology allows people to communicate regardless of time or location, giving rise to a raft of contemporary etiquette concerns. Foremost among these concerns is consideration for the sensibilities of those in our physical presence when we take a call. This article offers guidance to the bewildered.

1) It is a truth universally acknowledged that cell phones must be switched off in the theatre. There is absolutely no excuse. Offenders shall be tarred and feathered. Obviously, this also applies to the cinema, the symphony and performance art. Rock concerts and hip-hop shows are generally considered exempt, however, a punter with his fingers in his ears screaming "Huh? Huh? Huh?" into his cell is a frightful sight.

2) When piloting an automobile, use a hands-free device or resist answering incoming calls. Not only is it dangerous to talk and drive, but it is illegal in many countries. Care should be taken not to incite road rage in other motorists. Furthermore, chatting vacuously on your cell while mounting the footpath will pique pedestrians.

3) Conducting loud cell phone conversations on public transport should be avoided at all costs. To believe that other commuters ought to be interested in your conversation is narcissistic at best, to subject travelers to your confabulation is an indulgence.

4) When in the company of others, neither take nor make telephone calls. Nothing is more irksome than being spurned by a friend whose frequent cell phone conversations take precedence over live chats. Answering an incoming call in an interview or business meeting is to be avoided at all costs.

To observe basic cell phone etiquette is neither difficult nor inconvenient. Technology such as cell phones creates many possibilities for the advancement of society; society is founded upon mutual regard for one another. Always refer to the fundamental principle of good manners: Treat others as you yourself wish to be treated.

UNIT 12

Job Interviews

Learning Objectives

After learning this unit, you will be able to:
- understand different types of job interviews;
- analyze situations of job interview communication regarding interview questions and interview etiquette;
- prepare for a job interview;
- write a resumé.

Section I Warm-Up

1. When you graduate, you must face an important problem of finding a job. Which aspect of a job will attract you most?

   _____
   _____
   _____
   _____

2. Describe your ideal job.

   _____
   _____
   _____
   _____

Section II Points to Remember

There are important points to remember and some rules to follow in present-day international communication. The following is a summary of the basics in regard to types of job interviews, how to prepare for a job interview, interview etiquette and writing a resumé. Referring to these points constantly may help you prepare for a job interview well.

Part 1 Definition and Types of Job Interview

1. **Definition**
   - A job interview is a process in which a potential employee is evaluated by an employer for prospective employment in his/her company, organization, or firm.

2. **Types of Job Interview**
   1) Behavioral Interview
      - Past-oriented.
      - Testing points: team spirit, leadership or creativity.
      - The STAR method: situation, task, action, and result.

UNIT 12 Job Interviews

2) Group Interview and Tips
   - Be polite to other interviewees throughout the interview.
   - Be alert and ready for anything.
   - Listen carefully. The interviewers will usually give an overview as well as detailed instructions.
   - Be considerate. Interviewers may be looking for someone with leadership skills, but this does not mean you have to talk over others or try to be the loudest.
   - Give others a turn. Again, if you want to show leadership, delegate tasks to others. Don't try to do it all yourself.
   - Make eye contact with people at some point.
   - Invite quiet people. If someone doesn't say much, ask for their opinion.
   - Praise others for their good ideas.
   - Don't be shy. Speak out, but don't cut other people off or go over your allotted time for the question or exercise.

3) One-on-One Interview

4) Telephone Interview

   It takes place if a recruiter wishes to reduce the number of prospective candidates before deciding on a shortlist for face-to-face interviews.

5) Panel Interview
   - Presentation format.
   - Role format.
   - Skeet shoot format.

6) Stress Interview
   - Working overloaded.
   - Dealing with multiple projects.
   - Handling conflicts.
   - Handling pressure.
   - Emotional responses.

Part 2 How to Prepare for a Job Interview

- Search the company on the Internet.

- Find the position details and read them well.
- Prepare a two-minute introduction summarizing your education, your experience, your career goals and how this position will fit into your future plan.
- Review your resumé.
- Prepare several copies of your resumé, references and any pertinent work samples.
- Dress in a clean and conservative business suit.

Part 3 Interview Etiquette

- Arrive at least 15 minutes before your interview.
- Make a positive and professional first impression by being assertive, giving a firm handshake to each interviewer and addressing each interviewer by name as he or she is introduced.
- Keep fine postures and smile. When you smile, you'll look more relaxed and confident.
- Speaking clearly to reinforce your professionalism and your ability to communicate effectively.
- Use technical terms only when answering relevant questions.
- Ask questions if you don't understand.
- After the interview, shake each interviewer's hand and say their names as you thank them.

Part 4 Writing a Resumé

1) A resumé establishes a first impression of a potential job candidate's skills, background and employment value.
2) A resumé always includes the following components:
   - Personal information.
   - Work experience.
   - Education.
   - Additional skills.
   - Other accomplishments.

Part 5 Essentials for a Chinese

The following are some rules to remember when you attend a job interview:
- Understand different types of interviews and common interview questions.
- Prepare well for the job interview.
- Be polite in the job interview.
- Don't interrupt others.
- A good resumé helps a lot.

And you can add more…

Section III Let's Do It!

Activity 1 Answering a Behavioral Interview Question

Behavioral interviews are past-oriented in that they ask interviewees to relate what they did in the past. Questions asked in a behavioral interview have some testing points that measure team spirit, leadership or creativity. Can you give an example of how you effectively worked with other people to accomplish an important goal?

_____
_____
_____
_____
_____
_____

Activity 2 A Presentation on the Preparation of a Job Interview

Prepare a three-minute speech entitled "How Should We Prepare for a Job Interview?" Present your speech in a small group of 4-5 people. The best in the group should go to the front and make the speech to the class. You can write down keywords or outline of your speech in the space below.

How Should We Prepare for a Job Interview?

Beginning:
_____
_____
_____

Body:
_____
_____
_____
_____

Ending:
_____
_____
_____
_____

Activity 3   Dos and Don'ts for a Job Interview

Discuss in a group to sum up some dos and don'ts of a job interview and fill in the table.

Dos	Don'ts

Activity 4   A Job Interview Role-Play

Role-play a job interview. One student acts as an interviewer. The other plays the role of an interviewee.

UNIT 12 Job Interviews

Student A's Cue Card:

You are going to attend an interview for the position of assistant general manager of a hotel. The interviewer may ask you the following questions:
- Your expected salary
- Your work experience
- Your qualifications
- Your strengths and weaknesses
- Your career ambitions
- Your personal qualities
- Your interests

Ask the interviewer the following questions:
- Work place
- Benefits of the job
- Promotion opportunities
- Working hours
- Job responsibilities

Student B's Cue Card:

You are going to interview an applicant for the position of assistant general manager of a hotel. Ask him/her the following questions:
- His/her expected salary
- His/her work experience
- His/her qualifications
- His/her strengths and weaknesses
- His/her career ambitions
- His/her personal qualities
- His/her interests

The interviewee may ask you the following questions:
- Work place
- Benefits of the job
- Promotion opportunities
- Working hours
- Job responsibilities

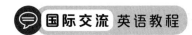

Activity 5 Writing a Resumé

1. What components should a resumé include? Discuss with your partners and write them down.

   _____
   _____
   _____
   _____

2. Write your own resumé.

Activity 6 Listening About Bad Job Interviews

Listen to the audio "Bad Job Interviews", and answer the following questions.

1) According to the report, what can an interviewee do during an interview?
2) Which word do we use to describe interview questions that are not relevant to the job?
3) According to interviewee Olivia Bland, the interviewer criticized her body language but not the way she sat. Is it true or false?
4) What can protect an interviewee from being treated unfairly and being asked questions that aren't relevant to the job?
5) What interview questions can be annoying?

UNIT 12 Job Interviews

Section IV Tool Box

1. Useful Words and Expressions
   1) Describing Yourself
      - 适应性强的 adaptable
      - 主动的，活跃的 active
      - 有雄心壮志的 ambitious
      - 有理解力的 apprehensive
      - 有能力的 capable
      - 能胜任的 competent
      - 有合作精神的 cooperative
      - 富有创造力的 creative
      - 有奉献精神的 dedicated
      - 勤奋的 diligent
      - 坚定的 determined
      - 守纪律的 disciplined
      - 尽职的 dutiful
      - 有效率的 efficient
      - 精力充沛的 energetic
      - 忠诚的 faithful
      - 直率的 frank
      - 宽宏大量的 generous
      - 幽默的 humorous
      - 公正的 impartial
      - 有才智的 intelligent
      - 条理分明的 logical
      - 谦虚的 modest
      - 坚持的 persistent
      - 严守时间的 punctual
      - 负责的 responsible
      - 性情温和的 sweet-tempered
      - 孜孜不倦的 tireless

2) Position
   - 董事长 president
   - 总经理 general manager
   - 总监 director
   - 主管 supervisor
   - 秘书 secretary
   - 助理 assistant
   - 协调人 coordinator
   - 代表 representative
   - 客服 account
   - 文案 copywriter
   - 会计 accountant
   - 出纳 cashier
   - 分析师 analyst
   - 专家顾问 consultant
   - 设计师 designer
   - 策划 planner
3) Department
   - 行政部门 Administration Department
   - 运营部门 Operation Department
   - 执行部门 Execution Department
   - 生产部门 Production Department
   - 财务部门 Financial Department
   - 广告部门 Advertising Department
   - 业务部门 Business Department
   - 质量监督部门 QC (Quality Control) Department
   - 信息技术部门 IT (Information Technology) Department
   - 人力资源部门 HR (Human Resources) Department
   - 销售部门 Sales Department
   - 技术部门 Technical Department
   - 市场部门 MKT (Marketing) Department
   - 公关部门 PR (Public Relations Department)
   - 产品部门 Product Department

UNIT 12 Job Interviews

- 企划部门 Planning Department
- 采购部门 Purchasing Department

2. **Useful Sentences**

   1) Interview Questions
      - Tell me about yourself.
      - What are your strengths/weaknesses?
      - What do you see as a major success in your life?
      - Describe a major disappointment in your life.
      - What does success mean to you?
      - What are three of your greatest accomplishments?
      - What are your plans for the future?
      - Have you done any volunteer work?
      - What do you like to do in your spare time / free time?
      - Tell me about your educational background.
      - What academic courses did you like the most / the least?
      - Do you have plans for further education?
      - Why did you choose your major?
      - Why do you want this job?
      - Why should we hire you?
      - Why do you want to work for our company?
      - Why did you leave your previous job?
      - Can you describe your previous jobs?
      - Can you multi-task?
      - How do you feel about learning new things?
      - Have you ever had trouble with a boss? How did you handle it?
      - What are your salary expectations?
      - Do you work well with others?
      - What strengths would you bring to a team?

   2) Communicating with Job Interviewers
      - It is really my honor to have this opportunity for an interview.
      - I am coming for your advertisement for...
      - I believe that I am qualified for this job.
      - I am looking for a job that better suits my talents and allows me to challenge

myself constantly.
- If you offer me the job, how soon would you want me to start?
- When could I expect to hear from you?
- Are there any further steps in the interview process?
- What are the major responsibilities of this position?
- Are there possibilities for promotion?

Section V Do You Know?

Supplementary Readings

Read the following two passages and find out more about job interviews. The answers to the questions at the beginning of each passage can be found through reading.

Passage 1 How to Prepare for a Job Interview in English

Questions:
- What does the preparation include?
- What should you do if you find yourself struggling to answer a question?
- What should you pay attention to when you role-play an interview?
- Is body language important in a job interview?

How should you prepare for an interview, if English is not your first language? The British Council's Megan Oliver shares a few tips.

Preparation Is Key

Prepare for your English job interview just as you would for any other interview. This may include searching the organization's history and mission, determining the travel time needed to get to the interview location, organizing your materials and choosing an outfit.

UNIT 12 Job Interviews

Some companies may require you to take an English skills test during your interview, such as the British Council's Aptis. To help you prepare at little or no cost, several websites offer free online English skills tests.

Anticipate Potential Questions

Most interviewers have a list of questions to determine whether you would fit the position and organization. Sample questions might include:
- How would you describe yourself?
- What are your strengths?
- What are your weaknesses?
- Why do you want to work here?

Take some time to determine how you would answer these and other interview questions in English, and be prepared to provide real-life examples that relate to your job history. Refer to the job advertisement itself for keywords and ideal candidate qualities that you can highlight. Avoid memorizing your answers in order to sound as natural as possible during the interview.

If you find yourself struggling to answer a question, do not be afraid to ask the interviewer to repeat or reword their question. This is completely normal, and happens in many interviews between fluent English speakers.

Role-Play the Interview

One way to practice your language skills is to role-play the interview. Find an English-speaking friend who can act as the interviewer by reciting sample interview questions in English, and providing feedback on your answers. Alternatively, record yourself (on your mobile phone, computer or other recording device) asking and answering the questions in English. Play back the recording to see how you can improve your responses.

During your role-play, pay attention to the speed and clarity of your speech to ensure that your answers are properly delivered and comprehensible. Individuals tend to speak faster when nervous, so by practicing speaking slowly and clearly during the role-play, you will feel more relaxed and confident during the actual interview.

Don't Underestimate the Importance of Body Language

Psychologist Dr. Albert Mehrabian suggests that only 7% of communication

involves spoken word. According to Dr. Mehrabian, 55% of communication is based on non-verbal behaviours (like posture and eye contact), and 38% is based on tone of voice.

It's unlikely that your interviewer will penalize you for pronouncing a word incorrectly. By ensuring that you speak with confidence during the interview, you can make a positive impression.

Being Multilingual Is a Major Asset

In today's global job market, the ability to speak multiple languages in the workplace is a major asset. According to a report by *New American Economy*, the number of online job postings targeting bilingual workers has more than doubled between 2010 and 2015. Job recruiters are actively seeking individuals who understand more than one language, so you can rest assured that your language skills will be valued.

Learning a new language takes patience and dedication, two traits that can set you apart from other job applicants right from the start. You can even consider sharing your language-learning story as an example of the skills and personal qualities you can bring to the organization.

Passage 2 What Are the Top 10 Skills That'll Get You a Job When You Graduate?

> **Questions:**
> - What do graduate employers place a lot of emphasis on?
> - What is commercial awareness?
> - How can you describe your skills on your CV?

Have you got the key skills graduate employers look for? You'll need to give examples of these essential competencies in your job applications and interviews to impress recruiters and get hired.

Graduate employers place a lot of emphasis on finding candidates with the right skills and competencies for their organizations. Depending on the career sector and profession you choose to work in, there could be very specific skills, abilities and knowledge needed to do the job.

These are complemented by the general competencies and behaviours that are essential for a successful career, which are the key employability skills—the core skills that will make you effective at work, whatever job you do. They are sometimes known as transferable skills because you develop them over time and take them with you as your career develops. Think of them as your passport to career success. You'll need to use your work experience to demonstrate these skills.

The Top Ten Skills Graduate Recruiters Want

1) Commercial Awareness (or Business Acumen)

This is about knowing how a business or industry works and what makes a company tick, showing that you have an understanding of what the organization wants to achieve through its products and services, and how it competes in its marketplace.

2) Communication

This covers verbal and written communication, and listening. It's about being clear, concise and focused, and being able to tailor your message for the audience and listening to the views of others.

3) Teamwork

You'll need to prove that you're a team player but also have the ability to manage and delegate to others and take on responsibility. It's about building positive working relationships that help everyone to achieve goals and business objectives.

4) Negotiation and Persuasion

This is about being able to set out what you want to achieve and how, but also being able to understand where the other person is coming from so that you can both get what you want or need and feel positive about it.

5) Problem-Solving

You need to display an ability to take a logical and analytical approach to solve problems and resolve issues. It's also good to show that you can approach problems from different angles.

6) Leadership

You may not be a manager straight away, but graduates need to show potential to motivate teams and other colleagues that may work for them. It's about assigning and delegating tasks well, setting deadlines and leading by good example.

7) Organization

This is about showing that you can prioritize, work efficiently and productively, and manage your time well. It's also good to be able to show employers how you decide what is important to focus on and get done, and how you go about meeting deadlines.

8) Perseverance and Motivation

Employers want people to have a bit of get-up-and-go. Working life presents many challenges and you need to show employers that you're the kind of person who will find a way through, even when the going gets tough...and stay cheerful.

9) Ability to Work Under Pressure

This is about keeping calm in a crisis and not becoming too overwhelmed or stressed.

10) Confidence

In the workplace you need to strike the balance of being confident in yourself but not arrogant, but also have confidence in your colleagues and the company you work for.

More Key Skills Graduate Recruiters Look for

Think you've got the top 10 covered? If you can show your mastery of the other five key skills—managing ambiguity, resilience, analytical skills, entrepreneurial skills and IT skills—you'll be even better placed to land the graduate job you want.

1) Managing Ambiguity

Our advice explains what is meant by managing ambiguity and why it is a particularly important skill in complex, fast-changing environments, such as the retail sector.

2) Resilience

Graduate employers look for resilience in their recruits because it enables employees to cope with change, problems and stress. Find out how to develop your resilience and how employers assess it during the recruitment process.

3) Analytical Skills

Analytical skills enable you to work with different kinds of information, see patterns and trends and draw meaningful conclusions. Analytical skills are often assessed using aptitude or psychometric tests.

4) Entrepreneurial Skills

Spotting gaps in the market, suggesting ways to improve processes, or coming up with new ideas are all signs of an entrepreneurial approach. You don't have to set up your own business to make use of your enterprise skills; many employers will be looking out for graduate recruits with these qualities.

5) IT Skills

The best way to demonstrate your IT skills to employers is to show that you have been able to use them to achieve something, and you can demonstrate this with examples from your studies, extracurricular activities or work experience.

How to Describe Your Skills on Your CV

Here are three tips to help you write your CV in a way that showcases your skills.

- When you are giving details of the skills you developed in a job, internship or work experience placement, reflect the competencies listed in the job description and give examples of the most relevant skills first.

- Use confident language to describe your skills, for example, by drawing attention to awards or praise your employers have given you.

- If you're struggling to find a way to write about your holiday or part-time jobs on your CV, remember that it's better to focus on transferable skills than routine tasks.